MW00565721

BROKEN SOLDIERS

THE MAKING OF HEROES

Authored By:
James D. Brewer

PublishAmerica
Baltimore

First printing

PublishAmerica has allowed this work to remain exactly as the author intended, verbatim, without editorial input.

Softcover 9781462641239
PUBLISHED BY PUBLISHAMERICA, LLLP
www.publishamerica.com
Baltimore

Printed in the United States of America

Freedom is never more than one generation away from extinction. We didn't pass it to our children in the bloodstream. It must be fought for, protected, and handed on for them to do the same, or one day we will spend our sunset years telling our children and our children's children what it was once like in the United States where men were free.

—Ronald Reagan—

This book is dedicated to those who died in the Vietnam War; to those who returned from the war but left something behind; to those brave ARVN soldiers who I fought beside, shoulder-to-shoulder, in the jungles, rice paddies, and mountain tops of III Corp, South Vietnam. I am certain that my life was spared more times than I ever realized because of their heroism and sacrifice, to them I am forever indebted.

A special thanks to my wife Maggie who has incessantly been my greatest encourager and who has always believed in me.

The actual writing of this book began September 2005

Table of Contents

Introduction 11

Chapter 1: We Are Not Home Yet 17
Taken 18
Broken 24
Betrayed 28
Hope 32

Chapter 2: In Country 42
The Beginning 42
Destination I-Corps, Democratic Republic of Vietnam 43
The Good News and The Bad News 49
Move Out Troop 53

Chapter 3: Welcome Home Troop 60
The Big Switch 61
Is It About Building Up or Tearing Down? 65
Combined Operations 69

Chapter 4: The Waiting Game 76
Hurry Up and Wait 77
Task Force 225 — In The Shadow of The Black Virgin 79
Journey Into The Unknown 80
Drawn Into The Snare 86

Chapter 5: Never Go Back the Way You Came .95

Out of Touch 99

Looks Are Deceiving—Perceptions Are Misleading.........101

Going Against The Grain 110

Don't Make Waves..114

To God Be The Glory..117

Chapter 6: The Black Hole................................121

The Awakening 121

Brokenness to Wholeness 126

Chapter 7: The Longest Night...........................129

Tet – 1971 129

Thanks But No Thanks 132

Another Day in Paradise 136

Lord – "Please Don't Let The Daylight End".................143

Zero-Dark 30..147

Chapter 8: Victory Denied.................................158

True Lies — Hidden in the Open...................................159

First American Casualties in Vietnam...........................161

Up Close and Personal...164

Hope and Forgiveness..169

Chapter 9: Ours Was a Just Cause.....................173

Hopeful Results..175

Locked Away...177

Chapter 10: The Long Road Home.......181

Lost and Found 181

Return..182

Finding Purpose 183

Chapter 11: So What's the Take Away?........186

Conclusion 186

Introduction

Have you ever heard the sayings, *"Old men start the wars, young men fight them"* or *"Rich folks start the wars, poor folks fight them?"*

Well, they weren't rich men and most of them were not old men; they were young men, many of them just fresh out of high school. They were the ones directly involved in the combat missions. They were loyal Americans, committed to the preservation of freedom. It broke their hearts then and it breaks their hearts today to see a society that ignores the sacrifices they made on the battlefield. We Americans take our freedoms for granted. We Americans basically ignore the sacrifices that the young men and women are making today to preserve freedom.

Until our latest armed conflicts in the Middle East, the Vietnam War, often called America's Longest War, was the longest military conflict in U.S. history. The hostilities in Vietnam, Cambodia, and Laos, claimed the lives of more than 58,000 Americans, another 304,000 were wounded. The Vietnam War was a military struggle fought in Vietnam from 1959 to 1975, involving the North Vietnamese and the National Liberation Front (NLF) in conflict with United States forces and the armed forces of South Vietnamese government. From 1946 until 1954, the Vietnamese had struggled for their independence from France during the First Indochina War. At the end of this war, the country was temporarily divided into North and South Vietnam. North Vietnam came under

the control of the Vietnamese Communists who had opposed
France and who aimed for a unified Vietnam under Communist
rule. The South was controlled by Vietnamese who had
collaborated with the French. In 1965 the United States sent
in ground troops to prevent the South Vietnamese government
from collapsing. Ultimately, however, the United States failed
to achieve its goal, and in 1975 Vietnam was reunified under
Communist control; in 1976 it officially became the Socialist
Republic of Vietnam. The capitol city of the Democratic
Republic of South Vietnam, Saigon, was renamed Ho Chi
Minh City. During the conflict, approximately 3 to 4 million
Vietnamese on both sides were killed; in addition another 1.5
to 2 million Lao and Cambodians who were drawn into the
war lost their lives.

The Vietnam War was the longest and most unpopular
war in which Americans ever fought. There is no reckoning
the cost. The toll in suffering, sorrow, in rancorous national
turmoil can never be tabulated. No one wants ever to see
America so divided again. And for many of the more than 3
million American veterans of the war, the wounds of Vietnam
will never heal. The losses to the Vietnamese people were
appalling. The financial cost to the United States came to
something over $150 billion dollars. If you calculate that into
2009 dollars the cost would be somewhere in the neighborhood
of $7.8 trillion dollars…. a staggering sum in terms of lives
lost and broken and in dollars lost and thrown away.

Direct American involvement began in 1955 with the
arrival of the first military advisors. The first combat troops

arrived in 1965 and we fought the war until the cease-fire of January 1973. To a whole new generation of young Americans today, it seems a story from the olden times. For those of us who fought the war, it does not seem all that long ago. Some of us still wake-up with night-sweats, we're awakened by the sound of incoming, or the poom... poom... poom of distant artillery fire.

No event in American history is more misunderstood than the Vietnam War. It was misreported then, and it is misremembered now. **Richard M. Nixon, 1985**

You should be aware that in addition to the more that 3 million American men and women who served in Vietnam, an estimated 43 million Americans; parents, brothers, sisters, wives, husbands, and children were directly affected by the losses in Vietnam.

As of May 2006 the names of the 58,253 men and women who were killed or remain missing are inscribed on The Wall. The average age of the young men who lost their lives in Vietnam was 23 and 61% of those who lost their lives were younger than 20 years of age. The Department of Defense is responsible for making decisions about adding names to the Memorial. Names are added annually in May, just before Memorial Day.

Those Vietnam veterans and veterans of all wars are loyal Americans; they are the true heroes that have sacrificed much. Many of them returned from the war wounded in ways that are visible to the eye. They bear scars left by bullets or shrapnel. Many lost eyes or limbs, wounds that are obvious to us.

There is however, another category of its own; there are countless numbers of wounded veterans whose names and statistics are not recorded in any After Action report. There are those veterans who were direct casualties of the war; however their names are not recorded on The Wall. Their lives were destroyed and they struggled to live with the weight of the invisible burdens they carried. Unable to bear the pain and the memories they could not cope with... tragically, they ended their own lives. There are also those veterans with invisible wounds who live among us, some lead productive, inconspicuous lives, some you see standing on street corners displaying signs that may say *Homeless* or *Vietnam vet, homeless, please help.*

This book is about cataclysmic experiences and the tragic loss of life and of the ruin of innocence. But more importantly, this book is not about me, it is about the transformation that can occur in our lives because of catastrophic, life impacting experiences.

Some of what you are about to read are accounts of the horrors I experienced with my fellow soldiers and the losses that were collectively suffered. Sooner or later we will all suffer tragedy. I pray that these stories and the message behind them will be life changing tales that will give you hope... if by chance, you are one of the *broken soldiers*. If you are not one of the broken, my wish is that these stories will help you to see in a different light, those seemingly incomplete human beings who have lost the ability to cope with life.

The personal experiences, which I am about to recount for you, have deeply impacted my life. I have been affected by these events in two ways. First, I have been hardened by the horrors of war and the aftermath of the taking of human life. I, as some of you, have seen humanity at its worst. I have seen communities turn against one another; family members all but disown one another because of their convictions over the war.

I have experienced the insanity of the total disregard for human life. I *was* the product of the Vietnam era war machine; the U.S. military trained countless thousands of young men to kill without discrimination. These young men, many of whom were barely out of high school, too young to vote, and too young to drink alcoholic beverages in their home town pubs, were asked to make split second decisions of who would live and who would die.

Our government spawned these soldiers, and set them in motion. Then, when they were finished with them, returned them to their communities. Many of these young men were seemingly unaffected by the horrors of war. Apparently the "military powers that be" discharged them with the assumption that they could and would lead wholesome and productive lives without the benefit of any form decompression and with not so much as one minute of counseling for re-entry to the human race. These young men went places most would never go. They saw things and experienced things that would make most grown men cringe or even cry. Most of us who have experience combat, up close and personal, are still haunted by those memories. It is unnatural to take another's life. We are taught as small children that human life is sacred. In Bible school we are taught to "Love One Another", Jesus told us that to love you neighbor as yourself is the second greatest commandment.

As for me, for many years I believed I was unaffected by the war. I had no visible or noticeable scars. After many years of my *"just get over it... I was there too"* attitude, my heart has been softened for those lost and *broken* soldiers. This book will not make any tragedy or losses go away as if it never happened, for you are never the same after a calamity. The softening that has occurred in me has been a process; it took a long time to take hold of my heart and mind. I am grateful and proud to say that now I have been transformed into a product of a God, full of grace, a God who loved me so much that he came to earth, allowed himself to be nailed to a tree, suffered, and poured out his life blood so that I would not have to endure an experience of unimaginable suffering and horror..... complete and total separation from God.

The process of change and redemption of my mind and soul is one that took many years.

My hope is that this book grips you and persuades you to compassion and compels you into action! Judge not, lest ye be judged and to follow the second greatest commandment: *"Love your neighbor as yourself."*

Chapter 1
We Are Not Home Yet

For Vietnam veterans and for veterans of all foreign wars who feel stung by not receiving a warm welcome home from serving your country, this book is for you. The lyrics from the Steven Curtis Chapman 2004 hit song, "Not Home Yet"; have deep and significant meaning to me in more ways than one.

We are all on a life journey here on earth. Our journey takes us on a very long and winding road. That road has many twists and turns. Along the road of life there are many forks. Which way do you go when you reach a fork? A famous saying comes to mind.... many of you are familiar with the name Yogi Berra. Yogi's claim to fame is that he was a Catcher for the New York Yankees during an era of the "Yankee Dynasty." Yogi played in 14 World Series and holds numerous World Series records including most games played by a catcher (63), most hits (71), and most times on a winning team (10). Yogi is also well known for his unforgettable ways of articulating many of life's situations. Regarding the road of life, during one of Yogi's many interviews a sports writer quoted him as saying, "When you come to a fork in the road... take it." He really had a way with words of wisdom, didn't he? The dilemma is when you do arrive at a fork in the road, which way do you choose to go? Most of us just make it up as we go. Sometimes our choices bring us results and sometimes our choices bring us consequences. It is simple, we make the choice and we will have to live with it. Yogi would say, "We made too many wrong mistakes."

It is a tough pill to swallow when we are forced into a situation for which we have no choice, in the matter or its outcome. Many of you were soldiers during the Vietnam War. Some of you voluntarily joined the Armed Forces. If you joined the Army you were considered "Regular Army", your service number began with an RA. Some of you were draftees, often referred to as "Unwilling Soldiers"; your service number began with a US. There should be no shame or dishonor for those who served during the Vietnam War, whether RA or US and no matter what branch of the Armed Forces you served in. A common myth is that most who served in the Vietnam War were draftees. Actually, more than two thirds of those who served in Vietnam were volunteers and 70% of those who were killed in the war were volunteers. Many of you were directly immersed in the combat arena, or you may have served on base camps in a support capacity. No matter what you Military Occupational Skill (MOS) was you are worthy and should stand proud. There should be no regrets for you because your country; its citizens did not greet you with a hero's welcome home.

TAKEN

I served in the U.S. Army during the Vietnam War. After graduating from high school I reached my first major choice in life. In other words, I had reached a fork in the road and I followed Yogi's advice, I took it, the proverbial fork in the road… I chose to not attend college and went directly into the workforce. I was hired initially as a bench hand, working in a tool and die shop. Since I grew up in the Detroit area and the automotive industry was booming, it seemed that I had made the right choice and could count on life-time employment at Gorham Tool Company and an eventual destiny to become a blue collar, UAW, middle class, card carrying Democrat.

After working for little more than a year in the tool shop I had worked my way up a bit on the pay scale and was working as a skilled Universal External Grinder and looking forward to achieving the next goal of becoming a Journeyman Tool Maker, life was good! Suddenly and unexpectedly my life and career goals were put on hold, I was involved in a very serious head-on automobile crash, one that nearly ended my life.

As I lay in a hospital bed recovering from my numerous injuries, I received one of the major shocks of my life. At the tender age of 19, I received a letter from the Selective Service System. It was an "Order to Report for Armed Forces Physical Examination." The letter addressing me by name began: *"You are hereby directed to present yourself for Armed Forces Physical Examination by reporting…."* I was both shocked and scared, what was I to do? There was a critical problem here; I was unable to report because of my injuries. My dear mother took charge and contacted the draft board, informing them of my dilemma. Of course her phone call alone was not enough to satisfy them; they still insisted that I report to the induction center for evaluation by Military physicians. My mother decided to talk with my attending physician to see if he would intervene on my behalf. The doctor graciously contacted the draft board and provided them with documentation of my condition and convinced them that I would be unable to present myself for a physical until my body had mended a bit more. Long story short, the draft board physicians kept tracked my progress in healing and eventually when I had mended enough to travel, the Army sent a vehicle and MPs to escort me to a Selective Service Medical Evaluation Board hearing.

After arrival and check in I was greeted by a First Sergeant for my first interview. The first words out of his mouth were, "Man, you really did get screwed up, didn't you?" Actually that is not a direct quote, but I choose not to put his actual expletive on paper. The result of the review with the First Sergeant and a group of medical doctors was that I would receive a 1-Y deferment. **Class I-Y** means: *"Registrant qualified for military service only in time of war or national emergency."*

During my period of recuperation I had arrived at a decision, I did not want to spend my life working in a tool shop. I had pretty much burned all bridges with the UAW Stewards in my shop. They warned me numerous times that I was working too fast; they labeled me a "Job Killer." Imagine that, black-balled for doing my job with too much eagerness! Well anyway, I had been raised to believe that in whatever you do, you are to work to the best of your ability. That lesson has continued to be a value of mine to this day. I was not about to compromise my integrity and be counterproductive to please the Union

Stewards. I decided a career change was the only way out. I investigated the types of jobs that were up and coming in technology, the kind of jobs that would be in demand in the foreseeable future. I decided to enroll at a technical school and over the next twenty-seven months, while still working full-time as a tool-maker, I earned a BA in electronics technology.

Close to three years later, still classified 1-Y with the draft board I reached another fork in the road of life. I knew that I needed a change in my life. For the past three years I had been working full-time in the tool shop, a place where I really no longer fit in, I was no longer one of the "brothers." I had been going to school in the evening full-time studying physics and electronics technology; additionally I was burning the candle from both ends with respect to my social life. I spent any precious free time partying like there was no tomorrow and cramming at exam times, a poor choice to say the least.

On a spur of the moment decision, seeing that once again, having reached another fork in the road, I took Yogi's advice. I contacted the local draft board and requested to be re-evaluated by the medical board. Soon after my phone call I received a second letter instructing me to present myself for a re-evaluation hearing and physical examination. My goal was to join the Navy on a program known then as "The 2-2-2 Enlistment." My reasoning for putting myself in the line of fire with the draft board was to continue my training in electronics while serving in the Navy. Much to my dismay the Naval Recruiter told me the "2-2-2" program was no longer available to me because their quotas had been filled. My only choice was to enlist for a six year stint with the Navy. I did a quick calculation on my fingers and figured that I'd be old by the time I served a six year hitch. At the time twenty-seven seemed "OLD" to me. That was not what I wanted to hear, but I had started the ball rolling and I had to live with my choice, once again it looked like another poor choice.

Needless to say I was found acceptable to serve in the Armed Forces and shortly afterward receive yet another letter from the Selective Service Board; this one however, was different from the previous two letters. This letter began: *"Greetings from the President of the United States, You are hereby ordered for induction into the Armed Forces of the United States, and to report at…"*

Consider this for a moment; are our lives a series of decisions or are our decisions based on destiny? In other words is it the choices we make in life that lead us to our destiny or is it our destiny that influences the choices we make? We are human beings made in the image of our Creator, God. He has created us and given us freedom of choice and if you really give some deep and contemplative thought to the question: What is the most powerful activity in which we engage?

I believe it is our power to choose. You may have instinctively decided to challenge me on this and I am here to tell you that you have already made a choice. Before you do anything in life you make a choice and if your choices are not wise, the outcomes will have powerful negative impacts on your life and maybe even on those close to you. On the other hand, if your choices tend to be the right choices, you may reap positive and powerful results from your good choices.

There are times in our lives where the power to choose is *taken* from us and we must live by the axiom that says you will, *"reap reward or suffer consequences"* of decisions for which we had or have no input, our voices were not heard! Choices that are forced on us are the most difficult to accept, especially when we suffer consequences or impacts to our lives. Where am I going with this? We do however; have choices in these circumstances, the ones where the choices were what we would not choose if the circumstances had not been forced on us. We can choose whether or not we **suffer impacts** or we **make an impact** on life. Choosing to make an impact can change your life and the lives of those we come in contact with. These impacts can be positive impacts in a big, big way.

My point here is that we can decide to wallow in our self-pity or we can turn a negative experience around to work to our advantage. I see it this way, no matter how much we are resistant to the choice made for us, it could be worse. We can train our mind to be grateful for the opportunity presented to us and accept it with grace. Behind every mountain or challenge in life there is a blessing, if only we muster the strength to climb the mountain. You may have heard the saying, "You can choose to be the victim or you can choose to be the victor." In my circumstance I chose to be the victor. I did not know the hard times I would experience the next ten weeks of Basic Combat Training (BCT) at Fort Knox, KY. I can't honestly say that during those ten weeks I was always the victor, but I did my best to keep a positive attitude or I may have been consumed by it all. In 1969 BCT in Echo Company was as tough as it gets.

BROKEN

I don't recall when it was I first became aware of the Vietnam War and our efforts to help South Vietnam achieve independence from Communist North Vietnam. I don't remember if I felt strongly one way or the other about my country's involvement in the war. The only real consideration I gave to the war was that if called I would serve. In reality I suppose I thought it wouldn't last long enough for me to get my chance. As it turned out I had nothing to worry about with respect of the war ending sooner than I would be able to serve.

Those of you who have served know how the rest of the drill goes. You were loaded onto a bus and taken to an armed forces induction center. After the induction physical and swearing in; you were whisked away to parts unknown to a life that had, for the most part, been entirely foreign to you. During those ten weeks we were no trips to the commissary, there was no after-hours socializing, only buffing floors, shining brass, spit-shinning boots and shoes, endless middle of the night flood drills and surprise fire drills, and of course drill sergeants and shave-tailed, butter-bar Lieutenants spitting in your face as they barked and yelled at you. You've been there, am I exaggerating? You were basically and summarily brainwashed and *broken* in order to ensure that, even under extreme duress, you would obey orders without question. You endured a physical training regime that pushed you to and even beyond your physical limits. The mental and physical conditioning was conducted by a cadre of seasoned and hardcore drill instructors who were expert at their trade. The guys who thought they were slick enough to con the DIs and shave corners and bend rules, found out soon that the DIs had dealt with the best of the best at that game. The slackers would soon find themselves smoked out and humiliated by the cadre. The skivers had earned themselves the torture of extreme physical tasks designed to break their strong-willed resistance to bend to the authority of the training cadre. If you've ever spent any time holding an M-14 in the "Dying Cockroach" position while a 2nd Lieutenant presses his foot on your stomach, you know what I mean when I say the physical training was at times, extreme! The training was difficult and sometimes even bit brutal. The intent of it all was meant to turn each pimple-faced, neophyte soldier into a lean and mean fighting machine…. that was their plan anyway!

Ironically I did not volunteer, but yet I was not exactly drafted. As it turned out I volunteered to be drafted.

Back in the summer of 1966 when thousands of young men, ages 19 to 25 were being removed from reality to the surreal world of life in the military, I received my first letter from the Selective Service Board. Our Federal Government had decided it was time to take a more active role in the war. Our military presence, in the form of foot soldiers actively involved in offensive combat operations, would be significantly increased from 184,300 to 385,300 troops. Subsequently the number of draftees was increased from that of 1965 in which we saw 230,991 young men inducted to 381,010 by year end 1966. In 1968 troop levels had reached an all-time high of 536,100, but the number of draftees had dropped slightly to 296,406. By 1969 when I actually volunteered to be drafted, the troop levels in Vietnam had decreased to 334,600 and the number of draftees reduced to 283,586.

The public anti-war sentiment had not declined; it had actually nearly peaked during 1969. There were protests against the war almost on a daily basis. College campuses were holding anti-war rallies regularly. May 4, 1970 was the day if the infamous the "May 4 Massacre" also known as the Kent State massacre. The shootings occurred at Kent State University in the city of Kent, Ohio. The tragic incident involved the shooting of unarmed college students by members of the Ohio National Guard. The guardsmen fired 67 rounds over a period of 13 seconds, killing four students and wounding nine others, one of whom suffered permanent paralysis.

By 1972 the estimated number of draft dodgers and deserters living in Canada had reached an estimated 70,000. Put all of that negative energy expressed openly throughout the general population of our country together with the extreme demands of basic combat training… it has a way of really bringing you down.

Out First Sergeant was a Cuban. He stood about 5' 6" in his combat boots, and his shape was similar to that of a fire hydrant. Form a mental picture of the cartoon character Tasmanian Devil wearing starched fatigues and Airborne Ranger jump boots, that's a picture of Sergeant Rios. He seemed to have no neck and I believe we never heard him speak in a normal tone. It appeared he could only communicate with us when he was shouting at the top of his lungs while a spray of spittle spewed in the face of anyone standing within range. During the ten-weeks of Basic Combat Training, Sergeant Rios did his level best, as did the entire training staff, to make our lives miserable. I am here to tell you, he succeeded and then some. I believe you could not find one member of Echo Company, Fort Knox, Kentucky, who would not concur with my evaluation of the quality and pain of our training.

By the end of most days we had double-timed ten-miles and more than a few of us had spent some amount of time in the *Dying Cockroach position, trying to hold our M-14 rifle up and steady while a Drill Sergeant or a Second Lieutenant stepped and stomped intermittently on our stomach. Can't ya just feel it, like it was yesterday? Did you ever tire of being called a snot-nosed-puke? Can you still hear your favorite Drill Sergeant shouting, "Look at guy standing next to you, some day you're gonna be stuffin' his sorry ass into a body bag!' 'Now listen to me you pukes… I'm tryin' to teach you somethin' and you better get it, right here and now!" I can hear Drill Sergeant Gethers as if it were yesterday. *Dying Cockroach Position: lying flat on your back, arms held up and above your head at 45º, legs held up and out at 45º.*

How many fire drills and flood drills did you go through in the middle of the night? Do you remember them? Now there's a real character builder! I don't know if all branches of the Armed Forces did these absurd and pointless drills, but I rather suspect that they all had versions similar to that of the Army drills. How many hours did you spend spit-shinning your combat boots, only to have a Captain or First Lieutenant step on them to scuff the shine? How did we ever get our hands and fingernails clean from endless hours of shinning our brass with Brasso? Do you still roll you socks and underwear as we did for foot locker inspections?

Dying Cockroach Position: lying flat on your back, arms held up and above your head at 45°, legs held up and out at 45°.

Those were the days! Then there was Advance Individual Training (AIT). All I will say about that is, it was much more bearable than Basic Combat Training.

BETRAYED

My father fought in W. W. II, he served as an Infantryman with the 5th Army from 1943 until 1946. His unit fought the Germans at Kasserine Pass and across Northern Africa in 1942 and 1943 then crossed the Mediterranean and invaded Italy at the beaches of Anzio. During the Anzio Campaign my Dad was wounded by small arms fire and shrapnel from a mortar round. His wounds were basically treated and bandaged and after a short recuperation he was put back on active duty and rejoined his infantry unit in combat. The battle raged on the beach head at Anzio for 4 months until the Allied forces finally captured Cassino, breaking the German resistance.

During the Anzio Campaign, the Allied forces suffered a staggering 29,200 combat casualties with 4,400 killed, 18,000 wounded, and 6,800 taken as prisoners or missing. There were an additional 37,000 noncombat casualties. Of the combat casualties, 16,200 were Americans (2,800 killed, 11,000 wounded, 2,400 taken as prisoners or missing) as were 26,000 of the Allied noncombat casualties. German combat losses were estimated at 27,500 (5,500 killed, 17,500 wounded, and 4,500 taken as prisoners or missing), figures very similar to Allied losses.

The Germans retreated to Rome, setting the stage for the next major battle to secure the area. My father's unit fought its way through Italy and France toward their ultimate destination, "The Mother Land" Germany. Shortly after crossing the border from France into Germany, during a Battle of the Bulge, my father was wounded again. This time it occurred in the Black Forest of Germany, he was wounded by German machine gun fire. The wounds were to his legs and they were severe enough that he was evacuated to a military hospital in Europe, and later moved to a U.S. Army medical facility, Percy Jones General Hospital, located in Battle Creek, Michigan. There he convalesced for several months and received rehabilitative treatment and this is where our government committed its biggest betrayal of my father. He was counseled and given the choice to remain on active duty or to sign papers that would release him from active duty status. By signing the papers he would agree to relinquish any disability benefits that he might be entitled to. Since his previous experience of being wounded and put back into combat, he chose to sign the papers.

When my father came home from the war at the ripe old age of 29 he was flat on his back with debilitating wounds to his legs. The wounds to one leg were so severe that the shin bone was replaced with an artificial, stainless steel bone.

My father returned to civilian life. He had a wife and a 3 year old daughter. The community welcomed him home, treating him like somewhat of a hero. After a period of recuperation he could get around and get out with his old buddies. He found his reintroduction to the "real world" a bit unsettling. He couldn't quite put his finger on it but things were not the same. Little by little he felt himself slipping away. Did he have a problem? Of course not.... he was a tough, war hardened soldier. He had recurring nightmares, but so did everyone who returned from the combat experience. How could he have a problem? A beautiful wife and sweet little daughter to welcome him home, even the community welcomed him home, how could he have a problem?

But the anxieties, anger, and resentment built up. Why didn't he just let it all out? He couldn't, he just couldn't let it out! There seemed to be no joy in his life, the nightmares accompanied by night sweats were still coming on him. He turned to alcohol; it helped him forget the nightmares and the terrible and inhumane things he has seen. Had he really been a part of it? The alcohol.... it helped him feel good, helped him... forget. It helped him laugh, while on the inside the canker burned. The more he drank the more of him slipped away. One minute he was angry inside and the next he felt empty, but the alcohol, it helped him hide it. He would not talk about the war, which seems to be characteristically common among war veterans who have experienced the horrors of combat.

What is the point of telling you of his betrayal?

The point is that because of the collective experiences of the horrors of war; the physical pain suffered; the betrayal of the government that he had served as a dedicated warrior, my father lost hope. He returned a shell of the man who had boarded the troop carrier ship at the port of New York City.

Perhaps you can relate somewhat to his story or perhaps you can relate to the way he felt. Did you relate? Do you feel betrayed by your government? You need to realize there is still hope. You need to reach deep and try your best to put it all behind you. You need to realize that there are perhaps thousands of veterans of war that feel the way you do. It is not a personal thing, put upon you by the military and your government. It is natural to feel the way you do. The path to recovery may seem impossible to you, but I am here to tell you it is possible to let go. I am living breathing proof of what I say.

You may say to yourself, "How can he be so sanctimonious? How can he know what I went through?" Well, I'll just turn that around and say, "How can you know what I went through?" Whose story is worse; who is hurting the deepest? My purpose here is to help you realize what I found.

HOPE

I have learned that with God all things are possible, even healing the wounds of the horrors of war and the aftermath of the betrayal that you may feel. Let go of it... just let go of it and read on with a positive attitude.

You cannot go back to the past, it is gone forever and you cannot change it. You can however, move forward and change a future that has yet to be discovered. You have the power to choose how your life story will play out. Do you want to continue to live your life with negative energies bottled up inside or do you want to live a life of integrity and joy? Remember that you can choose to be the victim or the victor, which do you choose?

I was a cynic; I had no patience with those who were not in control of their lives and their emotions. When I became aware of the negativity I felt toward combat veterans who seemed unable to get it together, I began to reflect on the kind of person I had become. Taking inventory of my life and my priorities, I discovered that I needed to reconsider my priorities and seek a new direction for my life. Although I did not realize it, for years I had pent-up negative energy inside of me. It had showed itself in varied ways over the years. Once God got hold of me and allowed me to see what was holding me back from being the compassionate and understanding person that I needed to be, it was as if a veil had been lifted from my eyes. I saw old self in the mirror and I did not like what I saw. I have since, discovered a passion in me that I did not know existed. This passion was lying in wait to be discovered. I became aware of my passion for writing and learning… but only after I was able to release the negative feelings I had bottled up inside.

Our sense of personal identity relies somewhat on our roles in life and the relationships we have. This can be a factor in how, philosophically, we understand ourselves. I was quite comfortable that, unlike many people, what I did to make a living and the sum of my material possessions was not "who" I was as a person. I discovered that I was only half correct in my assumptions about myself. What I did for a living very much defined who I was. What made come to that realization was that after more than twenty-seven years working as an engineer for one world-class corporation, I became a victim of the "downsizing syndrome" that began sweeping through corporate America during the middle to late 1980s.

I took my job loss very personally. I was embittered; after all, I had given my best and many times went above and beyond. My work ethic and loyalty to my employer was unquestionable. Having never missed a day of work in all those years, this was the thanks I got. My attitude was definitely soured. After a couple of months I found another job out of state. I came home every couple of weeks to spend time with my family. The extended time away from home was hard on my wife and children. After seven months I found a job closer to home, only a 90 minute commute from my home. It turned out to be the "the job from hell." My employer was a government contracting company. They were not only unethical, they had out-and-out lied to me about my job responsibilities and they had created a ghost department within our company that I supposedly managed. After a few weeks they were asking me to sign-off on time cards for people that I had never seen and who, to my knowledge did not exist. When I refused to sign the time card our relationship, which up to then had been cordial, became cold and stiff. After two months I had the misfortune to need major surgery and after my recuperation period, when I was to return to work, I was informed that my job had been eliminated, no surprise, but I again took it personally.

During the time I spent recuperating from the surgery, God got hold of me and slowly He revealed to me what my purpose was in life and He showed me that even though I considered myself a Christian and a follower of Jesus, I had been serving my Lord selfishly. I had been very actively involved in my church most of my adult life. "Wait a minute Lord!" Didn't that make me a good and dedicated Christian?

I came to realize that I had chosen exactly how I would serve and when I would serve. In other words, I remained in control. I had not surrendered myself to God. I was not a F.A.T. Christian (Faithful, Available, and Teachable). That is what He wanted from me and He also wanted to see in me the compassion and understanding that I had not displayed toward other, those who were emotionally unstable, or not in control of their emotions.

I had always been an avid reader of books; I mostly read murder mysteries and science fiction. While recuperating Christian friends brought me spiritual growth books. The two that helped me see myself through clear lenses instead of the rose colored one I had been using to gauge myself were "Practice of the Presence of God" by Brother Lawrence and "The Adventure, Putting Your Energy Into Your Walk With God" by Jerry Sittser. Those two books and a lot of prayer helped me find my passion. I saw that I was at that proverbial fork in the road once again. I saw that once again I had to choose. I recognized there was a need for change in my life and I had to either continue to live my life as a Luke-warm Christian or I could live my life as a committed Christian. I chose the hope of committing myself to what I was called to be and let God take control of my life.

I have met many Vietnam Veterans who still, these decades later, carry with them scars of the war and the sting of the rejection they suffered from the U.S. public on the whole. These deep emotional scars are the kinds that debilitate your spirit and ultimately your will to pull yourself up and out of the depression you have spiraled down into. Eventually the stress from the depression depletes you of your physical strength, too… from being surrounded by needs and demands… from being one of the too few carrying the too much. All of this has taken its toll in ways such as financial shortfalls, loss of relationships, and many other kinds of frustrations.

There is a prescription for broken and weary soldiers. In reality it is a preventive prescription. The prescription is a phrase, "Keep your eyes on Jesus so you won't get tired and discouraged." In other words, try your best to get your eyes off of yourself and the weariness and disillusionment you may feel inside.

Sometimes we carry our burdens on our shoulders. Those burdens sometimes become a chip on our shoulders. We look for someone to lay the blame on. We look at others who have problems in life and it seems that all we can focus on is ourselves. We even sometimes say to ourselves, "They have no right to feel that way, after all, look what has happened to me."Perhaps the recent public outreach to the soldiers of the wars in Iraq and Afghanistan has awakened a festering sore in you. I have to admit that I have caught myself feeling a twinge of resentment that I did not receive a hero's welcome home. My government did not reach out to me. Instead they whisked me through a physical that was so impersonal, so inept that they did not even acknowledge that I was seriously ill at the time. They didn't even send me home with my Good Conduct Medal and other medals I had earned and was entitled to. Instead, I had to fill out paperwork and send it in, then wait for the decision of a board to receive what was honestly earned and rightly mine! I, as many others returning from Vietnam, was rushed through the discharge process by a seemingly uncaring crew of military administrative and medical personnel. They were cold and callused as were the people I encountered in the airports I passed through on my quest to get home to my wife and my infant son. Can you relate to that experience? I know that many of you can.

Ask yourself this, "Whose sorrow is worse?" or "Whose pain is worse?" In reality, we all suffer loss during our lifetime. Loss can even come in waves, unrelenting for periods of time that may seem an eternity. Remember this, loss just like the seasons will come and they will go and like the weather, which is more often than not forgettable. Sometimes our losses can and may be forgotten. There are different kinds of loss and there are varying degrees of loss. The overwhelming ones are those that we will not let go of. As I said earlier, there are losses that we cannot forget, losses that will change us forever, but we must let go of the pain of those losses and get on with our lives. If we cannot let go we will remain victims and never become the victor over life changing events.

You may find it difficult to believe this, but I say to you that we need to experience difficult times in our lives or we will take for granted those times of happiness, joy, and blessings. I say this to you because I have suffered losses in my life. I am forever changed by the losses, but I have been able to let go of my anger and pain. No one will ever know the pain I have felt because of the Vietnam experience and other significant losses in my life, just as I will never have a true understanding of the pain you have suffered.

There is a special kind of weariness that comes with suffering. Jesus says in Matthew 11:28 *"**Come** to me, all you who are weary and burdened, and I will give you rest.*

Jesus' words here tell us that the weariness comes from carrying our burdens with us as we go through life. Our suffering from pain that we will not let go of is the ultimate cause of the pressures and stresses we feel each day. You may have gone through counseling for Post-Traumatic Stress Disorder (PTSD); you may currently be involved in some type of counseling in an effort to get your life back on track. I ask you.... "Have you tried Jesus?"

You're focused on the tasks, the "To Do" list that your counseling has established for you. You are convinced you that the act of checking off each item on the list will be your ultimate road to recovery. Still you know that you have not made any great advances. Now you blame yourself for the lack of recovery, your self-worth has begun to suffer again. Do you blame yourself? Do you blame others? Let me tell you, that your problems continue, not for a lack of trying and sincerity on your part.

You are struggling with problems that are bigger than you, bigger than your counselor is. Am I suggesting to you to discontinue your counseling? Absolutely not.... what I am telling you is to give Jesus a try. Give your burdens to Him and He will give you rest. We cannot overcome on our strength alone.

You see, when we go through life depending solely on our own strength, eventually we will run into obstacles that are bigger than we are. When we have come to the end our own might, our own ability to "overcome" what else is left?

If we have nothing else to rely on, we will be crushed by the obstacle, the event will become another disaster that will consume our strength and our ability to cope. Now we are in a place where we can find no happiness in life and we once again begin to struggle. That struggle may lead to bouts of depression and once again we become a prisoner, and again we become powerless to overcome the grip it has on our lives. These events, if treated with counseling sessions alone, are destined to repeat themselves again and again.

The Apostle Paul wrote something in Philippians 3:13 that I think is applicable here, "But one thing I do," he wrote, "Forgetting what is behind and straining toward what is ahead." If your goal in life is to achieve happiness, you will repeatedly suffer from disappointment, for happiness lasts only for the moment.

The Apostle Paul wrote about pressing on toward the "goal." If your goal is wholeness and joy in life then happiness will be a byproduct and you will not be disappointed my friends. Self-pity is a byproduct of the unachieved goal of happiness. You might be asking yourselves what my point is here. Now hear this, the point is a very crucial comparison of "Happiness" versus "Joy." Happiness is temporary because it is based on external circumstances. Joy is lasting because it is based on God's presence within us. Happiness is an unpredictable feeling; it covers it up discouragement, which is the root cause of many of life's problems: addictions, divorce, depression, and anger problems, just to name a few. Joy defeats discouragement.

You see, forgetting what is behind and leaving it in the past is what we need to do continually throughout lives. Surrendering the stress and pain of pent up anger, giving it over to God is what we need to do. God is the center of reality, God is the now!

Surrender is a word that makes us uncomfortable. Surrender and weakness seem to go together in our minds. Let me tell you, in the context of what we are focusing on, the very act of surrender takes an incredible measure of strength. If we surrender to God, contrary to our emotions, the act of surrender will liberate us from self-pity and will open us to a world that is much bigger and grander than we are.

Whether you want to believe it or not, we have choices in life. We can choose to be a victim of our choices. We can choose to continue to harbor bitterness because of the choices made by someone else and how they affected our lives. You may have returned from the war, but you are a casualty none the less.

Life, if we allow our minds to take this approach, can be an adventure. God created you and He wants only good for you. Many people think of God as legalistic. He is known for rules and for leveling judgment on the disobedient. Many think that a life focused on God is one of a mundane existence. Let me tell you, nothing could be farther from reality. Jesus provides us a portal to escape the ordinary and live our lives out loud, unashamed of being a follower of His in a world that is trapped by the very freedoms they seem to enjoy.

There is another thing I have learned in life and it is the most powerful thing we have in our lives. It is the power to CHOOSE. You are probably asking yourself why choosing is a powerful thing. Well, we have the power to choose this or that. We have the power to choose to go left or right. We have the power to choose to do right or wrong. And.... we have the power to choose whether to be the victim or the victor.

We all have something in our lives that challenges us. We don't always have a choice in our circumstances but we do have a choice in our destiny, choosing whether or not our choices end in results or consequences. Let me tell you friends... we are ALL eternal beings and we will all depart from this world, this life someday. Give it some serious thought.

God has given us the freedom and power to choose where we will spend eternity. What will you choose?

Chapter 2
In Country

THE BEGINNING

February 12th, this day had always been a day of significance to me. It was the day that we had always honored the memory of President Abraham Lincoln. When I was in grade school we colored pictures of Honest Abe and we recalled his many accomplishments. We even tried our best to memorize the famous Gettysburg Address. But now, after Vietnam, this day holds a completely different significance to me

It was a Thursday afternoon, February 12th 1970. The flight attendants of Flying Tiger Airlines had been pleasant and attentive, but even though they tried to be cheery and good-humored there was a noticeable attitude of detachment, an unintentional attitude that, I am sure, they were unaware of. The crew went through their normal routines for departure and take-off and once in the air and at cruising altitude, they busily went about serving their customers. It seemed like any other flight on any given day. But, there was an atmosphere of gloom and doom for the passengers that day. There was no first class section on this flight. The cabin was at full capacity but the passengers were not the everyday business class and tourist trade that the crew was accustomed to serving. As the airplane approached the runway for landing, there was a quiet nervousness throughout the cabin. I imagined that we all secretly hoped that the plane would not crash, after all, how could it end this way after having traveled halfway around the world to our destination? At the same time we were all hopeful that the pilot would receive direction to abort the landing, quickly regain cruising altitude, and return to Yakota, Japan, or better yet, Hawaii!

DESTINATION I-CORPS, DEMOCRATIC REPUBLIC OF VIETNAM

The flight from the United States had been basically uneventful. There were a few bumpy stretches and a couple of times we lost altitude, dropping suddenly and dramatically. Everybody panicked for a moment but the event was quickly forgotten, we had other things on our minds, I suppose.

We had departed from Fort Lewis Washington and after a brief stopover in Anchorage, Alaska we would soon be on our way again. On departure from Anchorage, which was bleak and frozen looking tundra, the pilot tried to make us feel special. After reaching our cruising altitude the pilot came on the public address system. He told us we were approaching the mountains and he would do his best to make certain that we all would get to enjoy the spectacular view. He flew out over the Alaska Mountain Range and tipped the plane, first to one side, then the other to ensure that all passengers had the opportunity to see the breath taking view of the ice clad mountain range and the tallest peak in North America. Mount McKinley was a majestic sight to behold, rising 20,320 feet above sea level. After the brief fly over we headed for our next stopping point, Guam. When we touched down in Guam we were allowed to briefly deplane and stretch our legs.

The airfield was a rather desolate terrain. The only thing of interest was the B-52 Bombers. There were what appeared to be dozens of them parked on the tarmac of the airfield. The gigantic aircraft looked sort of awkward with their extremely long, loping wings bent downward, almost touching the ground. The B-52 is a quite impressive aircraft. It is a long range bomber that has been in service for decades and they can drop their payload with surprising and impressive accuracy. Many of the B-52 airstrikes in Vietnam were flown out of this very airbase in Guam. Perhaps one of these impressive aircraft would, someday, deliver a sortie or ordinance for me... more on that in a later chapter

From Guam we headed to Yakota AFB, Japan where again we were allowed to briefly deplane to a holding area surrounded by a very high chain link fence. Men milled about, some smoking cigarettes and exchanging thoughts with newfound friends; while others stared off into space... recalling perhaps loved ones, or more likely, dreading the unknown fate that awaited them. I had a sort of sick and uneasy feeling in my stomach. I suppose each of us had his own mental picture of what lay ahead of us, but remarkably there was little if any sharing of the nervousness and trepidation that was felt throughout the group of young men.

The next leg of our trip would take us to our destination, Cam Ranh Bay, in northern part of the Democratic Republic of South Vietnam. As the plane approached the airfield you could see the airstrip and the nearby military installation. It was a collection of tin roofed buildings and sandbagged bunkers.

The landing was a precision, perfect three-point touchdown. I imagined that the pilot was a former ace Navy pilot who had landed fighter jets on the decks of aircraft carriers or perhaps a retired Air Force pilot who had run many B-52 bombing missions over Hanoi or had landed huge cargo planes on airstrips in places all over the globe.

The flight attendants scurried about and seemed to be a bit nervous as they prepared the cabin for flight arrival. My stomach muscles began to tighten and again that sick and uneasy feeling began to come over me.

The cockpit crew and the flight crew stood by that exit door as we deplaned. Some of us exchanged pleasantries with the flight crew. They wished us well as we passed by them, but I imagined that as they looked at us, subconsciously they viewed us as if we were ghosts, because the macabre reality was that many of us would make our final journey home in an airplane, perhaps even this one that brought us all this way from the other side of the world. But that journey back home for some of us would be on the inside of an aluminum box, a Government Issue casket draped with the flag of the country we had served and made the ultimate sacrifice for.

The stairway to the tarmac seemed to be abnormally steep and unusually long, it seemed to visibly stretch like the special affects you would see in a movie. I felt as though I was walking into a dream, or should it more appropriately be described as a nightmare. At this point in my young life, this was probable the most surreal experience I had ever e encountered.

During our Army Advanced Individual Training (AIT), we had been told that Vietnam was hotter than the fires of hell. But as I stepped out of the plane, I thought to myself that the Drill Sergeants had under stated the intensity of the heat, and the air….. it seemed so thick that you could cut it with a knife!

The next thing I noticed was an unfamiliar smell…… what was that repulsive and overpowering stench? It seemed to fill your nostrils with an almost smothering odor. In the distance I could see what appeared to be a base camp comprised of seemingly endless sandbagged bunkers and two story, tin roofed, wooden barracks buildings. The whole compound and many structures were surrounded by several perimeters of razor wire. Off in the distance I could see palm trees and lush green mountains that sloped down to a beautiful bay that opened to a large body of water, which I would later realize was the South China Sea.

What was wrong with this picture? On one hand it looked like a resort area with its white sands beach and palm trees, yet my mind told me I was definitely in a war zone.

I noticed black smoke that spiraled into the sky. Later I learned the origins of that unforgettable disgusting odor and the black smoke; it came from burning human excrement. The unlucky ones, soldiers who had broken rules, carried out the daily chore of mixing diesel fuel with human waste and setting fire to the disgusting blend. Those rules would soon be barked out at us by a not so gentle hard-nosed sergeant who was pissed off at the world that his distinguished career had come to this, baby sitting a bunch of snot nosed pukes, half terrified newbies who had no clue of what lay ahead for them. The sergeant was also pissed off that at least a third of the dumb young faces that stared at him would, at some point over the next 12 months, be zipped into body bags and shipped off to graves registration before they took their final ride home that shiny aluminum coffin to a country that could care less about them and cared even less about the mission to which they had been assigned. In fact, the sentiment of what seemed to be the majority of the civilians in the U.S., "those in the know", was that these fresh faced soldiers and the veterans returning home should be despised and looked upon with distain. They would be spat upon by shrieking women shouting "baby killer!", "war monger!" Many would just ignore them and the sacrifices they had made for a freedom taken for granted.

Here I was, a green, wet behind the ears buck sergeant, who just a year before had been a draftee standing in the induction center in Detroit Michigan, scared and repentant that I had not finished college because I thought the load of working full-time and going to school was just too hard. Little did I know then, where that life-changing decision would lead. I was on a journey with no destination in mind….. this journey however, was one that appeared to be a journey of no return.

We received our in-briefing and next we were assigned to our barracks, AKA (hooch). After a night of restless sleep I awoke to the sound of distant gunfire and the familiar sound of exploding artillery shells. I quickly went outside to see what was going on. Off in the distance I saw clouds of smoke rising from one of those majestic and beautiful mountains that sloped down to the white sands beach of the bay. There was a firefight and it was fully engaged. I could hear a distant and continuous sound; "pump, pump, pump." It was the familiar and unforgettable sound of a far-off artillery battery, firing sortie after sortie. They were delivering high explosive ordinance, hopefully dropping the artillery rounds right on top of the bad guys.

After breakfast, I decided to go take a shower and clean up before the morning formation. I walked over to the shower house. It was gray wooden building with a generous amount of high, screen windows. It was also a painfully public place with multiple showerheads and no walls for privacy. After turning on the shower and letting the water run over my head and body, I soaped down and then stood under the shower head, eyes closed, while I began to rinse. I was lost in a day dream while the warm water streamed over my face and body, it felt soothing and refreshing. I almost forgot where I was, remembering days gone by. Not so long ago I had enjoyed warm showers in the safe sanctuary of my home, back in Michigan. Suddenly I could feel a presence.... I opened my eyes and after a brief moment my vision cleared. There I saw standing in front of me two Vietnamese women, commonly referred to as Hooch Bas. They stood there, smiling and staring at me as if taking inventory. When they realized that I had noticed them, they giggled and quickly went about their business of cleaning up and straightening the shower house. I later learned that this was a common occurrence, something

that one should not get their proverbial shorts in a wad over.....
just get over it and get on with it!

If you've been there, you get the picture.... right?

THE GOOD NEWS AND THE BAD NEWS

After recovering from the shocking surprise in the
shower house I went back to the hooch and made my bunk,
straightened things before inspection, and then fell out for
morning formation. The morning formation was the somewhat
dreaded occurrence that was a part of the beginning of the
typical military day for a trainee or a newbie: **definition;**
(**newbie** or **newcomer**: *1. One who has recently come to a
community; a recent arrival. 2. A new participant in some
activity; a neophite*).

After barking orders for the day and assigning the group
alphabetically to chores for the day, the Staff Sergeant called
out six names, mine being one of the six. We were directed to
follow him to the headquarters office for further information
and instruction.

We went directly to the headquarters office where we were
told to wait until the base Commanding Officer (C/O) would
be able to speak with us. We stood for what seemed to be an
eternity; my mind began to drift into a daydream. Was this
good news? Had we suddenly been given a reprieve? Was
this the end of the bad dream? Had there been a mistake and
the six of us were going to be sent home? Or was this the

bad news? We're be being assigned to some kind of a suicide mission from which there was no return? Words my father had once spoken came to me, he had warned me, he said, "Don't let them convince you to volunteer for anything, nothing good will come of it, for sure."

Abruptly I came back to full consciousness when a Corporal called out our names and escorted us into the C/O's office. We each saluted, announced ourselves then assumed the position of parade rest. The C/O responded with, "At ease men." He informed us that even thought our entire artillery battery had been assigned to travel to Camp Eagle, located at Phu Bi, in I-Corp; we were being reassigned to the Military Assistance Command Vietnam (MACV). The C/O went on to tell us that our orders would be delivered to us shortly, after which we would be transported to another location for further instruction and ultimately deployment to our final assigned destination. We were then dismissed with no additional explanation. That was it, no real explanation! What did all this mean? None of us had a clue! What the heck was MACV anyway?

Later that day, after completing our chores of policing the area picking up discarded trash and cigarette butts, we were then assigned to the ritualistic filling of sand bags, a chore I grew to absolutely hate while stationed at Fort Sill, Oklahoma. Filling sand bags seemed to be a part of everyday life for an artilleryman. Wait a minute....

FREEZE FRAME! Hadn't I volunteered to go to Vietnam in order to attend the Non Commissioned Officer (NCO)

Academy? And didn't I choose the NCO Academy knowing that after successful completion I would graduate as an Artillery Crew Chief and be promoted to the rank of Sergeant, which meant I would no longer have to fill sandbags? As a Crew Chief wouldn't I be able order subordinates to fill sand bags? What was wrong with this picture? I hated the dirty and uncomfortable job of filling sandbags, so much so that I would volunteer to go to this god-forsaken land. After all, didn't I know that ultimately all new recruits were going to Vietnam anyway? Hadn't every Drill Instructor I had ever met bellowed the same line that they repeated over and over again? It went something like this "You miserable pukes are goin' to Vietnam and I'm gonna teach your sorry asses some skills that might save your worthless lives, so listen up!"

So why not volunteer…. it would get me out of filling sand bags, wouldn't it? I decided right then and there, I must take charge of my destiny…. more on that later. Anyway, back to the story;

That same evening, in the base NCO club, we struck up conversation with a group of soldiers who were celebrating the completion of their tour of duty; they would soon be on their way home. We listened intently as they shared stories of the life and times of a soldier in Vietnam. I later asked them what MACV was and informed them that my orders assigning me to Camp Eagle as an Artillery Crew Chief had been changed. I was now assigned to MACV, whatever that was. They explain to us that we were very lucky because the MACV guys lived on a big Army base in Saigon where they all worked in air-conditioned buildings. They said we'd likely be pushing paper and typing memos or receiving, inventorying, and dispatching supplies.

I remember thinking at that moment that I must have been blessed for some undeserving reason. I don't recall if I gave thanks to God or not, but I was feeling much better about the future. The six of us celebrated in the NCO club that night. The next morning the decision was made in our small group of six that we must take control of our immediate situation. We reasoned that each of us had suffered through the academy so we would not have to do menial tasks and fill sandbags to boot!

We decided to take charge of our destiny and the way we would do it was; we were going to enjoy the rest of our days in Cam Rahn Bay and we weren't going to pick up someone else's cigarette butts and trash, we were going to unwind. After morning breakfast is when the work details were formed. We finished eating our morning chow and then we hid under the barracks, before morning formation and work detail assignments. After the area was cleared of cadre, we snuck off and hitched a ride on a military duce and a half truck that took us off the base. When we neared the water we asked the driver to stop and let us out. We spent the rest of the day swimming and relaxing on the beach on the South China Sea. The next two days were repeats of this day. Life was good!!

Move Out Troop

When we fell out for formation the next morning before breakfast, Sergeants Gary L. Brown and James D. Brewer were called out of the formation. We were told to eat breakfast then go directly to our hooch, collect our gear and report to headquarters. After we quickly gathered our things we walked across the base camp and reported to the base headquarters. Of course we had to sit and wait for the Commanding Officer (C/O) to return to his office. While we waited Gary and I exchanged thoughts on what our assignments might be. Of course we had no idea but we both assumed we would be working in some kind of office building at MACV Headquarters in Saigon. After a bit the C/O returned and we were ushered in to meet with him. After announcing ourselves and assuming the position of parade rest the C/O, who seemed quite bored with the whole thing, unceremoniously handed us our orders, which we read after leaving his office. With little to no time to completely understand what the orders said and meant we were told to load our gear and climb into a jeep. We were then escorted to an airstrip. After a short wait we unloaded our gear and we boarded a C-140 transport plane and after a bit we lifted off for parts unknown. We sat in the cargo hull of the transport plane which was about half full with other soldiers. It was a somber trip; no one spoke or interacted with others at all. After take-off I had time to read my orders again. They simply told me that I was assigned to the 25th ARVN Division, MACV headquarters at Duc Hoa. Duc Hoa… was that a place and where that heck was Duc Hoa.

Later that day we landed at Ton Son Nhut Air Base, Saigon, III-Corp. We were all taken to the Army base and dropped off in front of a building, which a sign on the front told me it was a Transient Barracks; a place that soldiers in route to where ever would sleep. A Staff Sergeant greeted us at the entrance to the barracks, he assigned us bunks and showed us were other accommodations were. Although we had not received work assignments, we believed this might be our final destination but to our surprise, two days later we were again summoned to command headquarters. Again we were directed to collect our belongings and wait in front of the barracks where a jeep would pick us up. We collected our gear and we were then escorted by jeep to the airstrip at Ton Son Nhut where we once again boarded a C-140 and lifted off, yet again, for parts unknown.

Shortly after take-off the plane reached what seemed to be cruising altitude, and then it began to descend. We landed on the airstrip and deplaned… we had no idea where we were, perhaps this is where we will be assigned. A jeep drove up to the plane and a Corporal instructed us to hop in. I introduced myself and asked the Corporal where the heck we were. He said, "Welcome to Bien Hoa Air Base. Gary Brown and I had no idea what the plan was and at that point we didn't care.

The Corporal delivered us to yet another Transient Barracks where we spent another two days. Gary and I were still in the dark as to our destiny, nobody seemed to be aware of where the heck we were headed and what we would do when we got there.

That first night was miserable. First we had to deal with fleas and after we finally got to sleep, we were rudely awakened by loud explosions. It sounded as if there was "in-coming" on all sides of us. Someone shouted that we were being fired on with rockets. It was complete mayhem, people running every which way without any direction of where we could take safe cover. Gary and I just ran into the courtyard and laid flat on the ground. That seems to be the best way to avoid being wounded by flying hot shrapnel. The attack ended as abruptly as it had begun. On returning to our hooch, I noticed my wallet lying open on my bunk. On inspection I saw that all my cash had been removed. I was robbed during a rocket attack, how low can someone be. I yelled in disgust at the top of my lungs, "Did anyone see who the low-life puke was who took my money?" No response, I was pissed!!

On the morning of the second day we were again summoned to headquarters, this by now was becoming repetitive and it was bordering on irritating. Each time we were summoned to headquarters, we were transported to another location. We were beginning to believe that we would never reach our assigned post. There we met with a First Sergeant; he informed us that the next morning we would be transported to our assignments as MACV Infantry Advisors to the Army of the Republic of Vietnam (ARVN). Infantry Advisor, what the heck is an Advisor? Going through the NCO Academy I was continually reminded by the Drill Instructors of how much money the Army was spending on my worthless behind. All that artillery training and now I was going to be an Advisor to a bunch of ARVN Grunts? Give me a break!!

The next morning after chow, we once again collected our gear, for hopefully the last time, and were again loaded into a jeep and transported to the airstrip. This time, however, we did not board a C-140; we were delivered to a heli-pad where Sgt. Gary Brown and Sgt. Jim Brewer boarded an Army helicopter, Bell UH-1, commonly known as a Huey. Other than the crew Gary and I were the only ones on board.

At this point my friend Gary and I had no idea of where we were going and we had no idea of what the job description was for an ARVN Infantry Advisor. All we knew was that we were headed for the ARVN 25th Infantry Division, wherever that was. Gary was headed for the 1st Battalion, 49th Regiment; I was headed for the 3rd Battalion, 46th Regiment. We did not know geographically where these fighting units were located, nor did we fully understand exactly what our assignments would be. We only knew that it must be "show time." No more shuffling, we were about to be introduced to the WAR and we were nervous.

I was the first to be delivered. The helicopter flew basically in a straight line at an altitude of about 300 feet for what seemed to be hours. The best I could tell was my sense of direction told me we were headed in a westerly direction to parts unknown. We flew over banana groves and rice paddies. Most of the landscape was heavily pock marked by bomb craters. We saw numerous villages that had been burned and destroyed. We could see the familiar footprint of areas where remote artillery fire support bases had been located, but still nothing gave us a clue of where we would ultimately end up.

Suddenly the Huey banked and we saw what was below. It was what appeared to be base camp that looked, from the air, to be incredibly small. I could see many sandbagged bunkers and what appeared to be an inner and outer compound separated by a greenish colored moat. The area around the base camp was mostly defoliated. It was a rural setting pockmarked by what appeared to be small craters caused by exploding mortar and rocket fire. It was obvious that "Charlie" had attempted, on more than one occasion, to take this base camp.

The familiar dikes of the rice paddies were the only thing recognizable in the surrounding landscape. I could see off to one side of the base camp and within the perimeter was a battery of 105 mm. Howitzers. I began to feel just a little bit at home since the artillery pieces were the only thing I had seen during the flight that had any familiarity to me.

As I write this, I can feel that unmistakable queasiness in my stomach. It is that sort of indescribable feeling of terror and nausea that you feel when you lay eyes on the needle, just before the dentist injects you with Novocain. Brace yourself for you know it is not going to be pleasant!

Imagine that you could recapture a moment of your life from the past. Which moment would it be? Would it be a happy time in your life that you could relive again and again? Or would it be a moment that you regret, one that you could undo or amend? How many of us haven't spent time reflecting on moments lost, all the time unaware that moments lost in regret are exactly that…. moments lost? If you could take a moment and make the most of it, shouldn't that moment be in the future rather than in the past?

Wouldn't it be fantastic if we could see a moment in our future that would change our life forever? We could make that moment rich and rewarding, if only we could see that moment coming. Have you ever wished or prayed for a divine moment? There are such moments in life if only we prayerfully seek them. They are moments where God reveals himself to us in such a way that it is undeniable. Divine moments are life changing in such a way that nothing will ever be the same again. If you could see that moment coming how would you prepare for it?

We have choices in life and we are all faced with defining moments in our lives. There are many moments in life, but the most important ones are the divine moments. What makes the difference in our lives is first we have to prepare ourselves for those unseen divine moments. Next we need to be aware of them when they present themselves. Most often we are not immediately aware of them, but instinctively we know that there is something different about these moments. They are moments where we must take action, even if with trepidation. Sometimes we will discover a divine moment wrapped in a mundane moment, just waiting to be discovered. When it hits us, it is an undeniable and almost indescribable moment.

If we do not act on those opportunities, they are forever lost. It's not to say that we will never have a divine opportunity again, it is just that the ones for which we take no action will never present itself in the same way again.

Revelation 7: 17 says in part, *"And God will wipe away every tear from their eyes."*

Why would we have tears in our eyes if we are going to spend our eternity in the presence of God our Creator? I believe it is at that time God may allow us to see the divine opportunities we missed in life, the times we could have made a profound difference in our lives or more importantly in the life of another. We missed the opportunity and it saddens us and brings tears to our eyes.

Soon my friend and brother, Gary Brown and I would be parting company. I did not know at the time, I would never see Gary again. I wish I could go back to those moments in time when it was just Gary and me. We were always together shuffling from one place to another, which brought us to this moment in time. I could have shared my faith with Gary; instead I wasted the opportunity given me. We spent our time having what we thought of then as fun. I look back now and see that it was time wasted. I can only hope now that before the end, my best friend, Gary made his peace and got right with God.

I must admit that at the time I was not walking the straight and narrow. Even though I was guilty of backsliding, I knew in my heart that I too needed to get right with God and start living my life differently. Why didn't I seize the opportunity? I regret it to this day.

Chapter 3
Welcome Home Troop

As the helicopter was about to touch down, I noticed a very young looking 1st Lieutenant standing on the helicopter pad, he waved to us as he braced himself against the dusty, violent backwash of the helicopter blades. After the helicopter came to rest on the pad, the Lieutenant hurried toward the chopper, hand outstretched to welcome his new arrival.

Inside the helicopter my friend Gary and I exchanged well wishes for each other... I remember it as if it happened yesterday, I said to him, "Good luck buddy, I'll see you on the other side, back in the real world". I gave him a quick hug and handshake; I then jumped out of the chopper with my gear. I wish I could relive that moment, it was too rushed. Gary was my best friend. As I look back now this unceremonious good-bye was just not enough for all that we had been through together...... Good-bye brother.

I grabbed the young Lieutenant's outstretched hand and we shook hands. We then quickly stepped back from the pad to give the chopper plenty of room to take-off. As it lifted off I waved to my dear friend Gary and the chopper crew. Little did I know that would be the last time I would see Sgt. Gary Lee Brown alive.

When we're preparing ourselves to go to Nam, we kept getting the reminders from the NCOs and Officers that some of us would return from the war in a box. Of course, deep down none of us really expected that it would be us that would make that trip home inside a shiny aluminum box..... or did we?

I can still hear in my mind the numerous times the drill instructors in boot camp and AIT would say you, "Look at the man next to you, you are going to be stuffin' that soldier in a body bag someday." "Do you wanna be the one who does sum-thin stupid that causes him to lose his life?" I used to hate hearing that! Were you ever in that situation? If you were, can you still hear in your mind, that relentless ragging? We heard it so much that we became numb to the meaning of the words that would ultimately ring so true for many of us. After all, bad things always happen to other people, don't they? Bad things always happen somewhere else in the world.

THE BIG SWITCH

I would not realize until a few month later that I had actually been assigned to the 1st Battalion, 49th Regiment and Gary Brown was, in fact, assigned to the 3rd Battalion, 46th Regiment of the ARVN 25th Infantry Division. The pilots of the helicopter mistakenly dropped me off first at the 3rd Battalion 46th Regiment.

We never really know when we will draw our next breath. I'm sure that you've heard it said that we should always live each day as if it were our last day on earth. Do we really live that way? Have you ever tried to live that way? When it comes right down to it, would you really know how to live that way?

When Gary and I parted on that helicopter pad, it never occurred to me that I might never see him again and I believe that thought never entered his mind either. Gary just loved to play pranks and have fun. I remember when we were in the flea bitten transient barracks at an Army base in Saigon. One evening we had spent too much time at the NCO club and had polished of too many beers. We left the NCO club; actually, we were some of the last to leave. We laughed and talked as we found our way back to the transient barracks. As we were about to enter the barracks, Gary pointed to an empty MP bus parked next to the building. We knew that the bunks were crawling with fleas, Gary pointed to the bus and whispered, "Let's go, we can spend the night in the bus." Sounded like a plan to me. We climbed into the bus and I made my way to the back and found a seat to curl up on. I quickly fell into a deep sleep. Gary, I assumed, did the same thing. Suddenly I was abruptly awakened by the cranking of the bus engine as it started up. I sat up suddenly and saw Gary sitting in the driver's seat. He ground the bus into gear and pulled out, turning on the road in front of the barracks. I said, "What are you doing?" Gary replied, "We're going for a joy ride." He headed straight away down the road; he made a quick left and another. We were heading down a straight-away when suddenly an MP stepped out of a jeep that was parked directly in the middle of the road ahead of us.

The MP put his hand up signaling for us to stop. He ordered us off the bus and into his jeep. All the way back to the barracks, he chewed on us about our joy riding in the bus. After we arrived, he escorted us into the barracks and told us that if he saw us outside the barracks before daylight, we'd spend the rest of our lives in the Brigg. Early in the morning, we were shocked from sleep as an MP yelled at us to get our butts dressed and get outside. We were then abruptly escorted to the C/O's office.

Hear we were again, waiting in the outer office of headquarters for the C/O to give us audience. This time there was no guessing, it was going to be bad news, we were definitely in hot water. Soon a PFC escorted us into the C/O's office. We again announced ourselves and assume a crisp position of parade rest. My head ached and my stomach churned. We received a good tongue lashing from the C/O and he made the usual threat of busting us, ripping the Sergeant's stripes from our shoulders, and on and on. I was almost biting my lip as it suddenly occurred to me that Gary might chime out with, "What're ya gonna do, send us to Vietnam?" It would be just like him to do that. Sometimes I thought he never had a serious thought in his head. What choices had brought Gary and me to this moment? I rather suspect it was a compilation of poor choices.

I once heard a radio talk show personality tell the story of a time when he was on the road making personal appearances around the country. On evening after a show he was making his way out to the lobby to meet fans and shake hands. He said that as he made his way through the crowd it was utter mayhem. He said he noticed a tallish young man with a walker. The young man had been trying to make his way toward the celebrity and had been literally pushed back against the wall.

The talk show host said he could see great disappointment on the face of the young man. The talk show host felt an instant compassion for the young man. The feeling of compassion compelled the talk show host to push against the crowd and make his way to the young man. The young man who was severely physically handicapped said to the man, "A doctor once told me that I would never walk, but look at me, I can walk." The young man said, "My family told me that I would never be able to write, but I keep a journal and I write poetry." Finally he said, "People told me I would never be able to hold a job, and look at me, I have two jobs and I work every day."

Isn't that encouraging? This young man, who had so much going against him, dreamed dreams and now he is living those dreams. He did not give up on life. He would not let the burdens of life bring him down. Instead he fought back with a strong will and a spirit of determination... he overcame. You too can overcome, but you have to dig deep and resolve that you will overcome. With determination from within and the strength of the Holy Spirit you can change your role from over whelmed to over comer, victim to victor. You need encouragement to do that though. There are people out there willing to help you and encourage you. You need not wait for them to come to you. You need to take action and go to them. Go to a church and get acquainted. There are good and caring people there who are sincerely waiting for YOU and they want to help YOU! Get connected, there are small groups that care for and support each other.

If at first you do not experience that community or the sincerity that I speak of, don't give up, go to another church and another and another until you find the help and care that I speak of. Just like in everyday life, everywhere you turn you can find insincerity. Insincerity exists in the Christian church too. Why? Because people are there! Wherever you find people you will always find those who live what they profess and you will also find those who put on a good front, that behind it lies insincerity.

"Insincerity is merely a method by which we can multiply our personalities." — Oscar Wilde

Please don't let that dissuade you from seeking out a place where you feel comfortable with the people of the church. Believe me, there are many more sincere Christians than the insincere posers. There will be someone who with help you and encourage you through you quest for wholeness.

Is It About Building Up or Tearing Down?

After the noise and settling of the dust the Lieutenant introduced himself saying, "Hi, I am Oscar and I want to welcome you home, this is the Tan My base camp." He said, "Are you a carpenter?... I sure hope so 'cause we have lots of work to do." I thought to myself, "This is a weird greeting." Ever since landing in Vietnam each day seemed strange, as if I was living in a surreal world. It was like a bad dream, one of those dreams where, try as you might, you cannot wake up;

your throat is paralyzed when you try to scream for help... no one can save you!

The lieutenant told me that he and the others were in the process of building a house. He explained that they had become sick and tired of living in a bunker made of sandbags and they were sick of the late night visits of the rats and tired of the never ending battle against the mosquitoes.

So, we were going to build a house <u>and</u> fight a war? Suddenly questions began popping into my mind but I was in a situation that was too new, too foreign to even begin asking questions. I decided to go along with whatever was happening until I could get a better picture of how I fit in here.

We walked up to the gates of the compound, my new home. ARVN Guards greeted us and Oscar introduced me to the men who seemed to be cordial and happy to see me. Happy to see me? Perfect strangers in this landscape that was so alien to me, like nothing I had ever seen or dreamed of, even in a bad dream. This was my new home; the realization still had not sunk in.

We walked on up the road leading into what appeared to be an inner compound with yet another guarded gate. Oscar introduced me to two more ARVN soldiers, guarding the gate. They were as equally cordial as were the guards at the outer gate. After exchanging pleasantries we walked into a partially finished building where two men were working, they were American soldiers. The men stopped what they were doing and walked toward me with outstretched hands. The first man, a tallish thin man with blonde hair, introduced himself, "Hi, I'm Captain Dave, pleased to meet you." The second man reached out his hand and introduced himself as Slater. He too was a young tallish, thin man with wiry blonde hair. He was a Staff Sergeant who, I would later learn, had served in Nam before; this was his second tour of duty. He'd been here before with the 1st Infantry Division, (The Big Red 1) back in 1966. He never talked much about it though and I learned later that this was a characteristic of those who had been engaged in intense combat.

There were still a few hours until dusk so work on the house resumed. I pitched in and helped in dismantling wooden 105 mm artillery shell boxes. We used the wood from the cases for inner wall covering and for flooring. We also used the wood to build some of the crude furniture we would use once the house neared completion. As the covering of the inner walls progressed we would fill the space between the inner and outer walls with dirt and gravel, the purpose being to slow down or stop bullets and/or shrapnel.

That evening after work had ceased, we gathered at a table for dinner which would be your choice of delectable C-Rations and a cold beer. During dinner, Capt. Dave informed me that the way they had conducted the advisory roles in the past, was that on combat missions we would take turns accompanying a company of ARVNs in pairs. First Slater and I would go out with an ARVN company on combat missions and when we returned Capt. Dave and Lt. Oscar would go out with a company. We would rotate in that manner every time there would be a company out on combat missions. There were, most times, one company of ARVNs out on search and destroy missions, one Company of ARVNs set up in ambush positions outside and around our base camp protecting from enemy troops and deterring mortar attacks, etc. There would always be two companies inside the base camp, one on stand-down, the other tasked with guard duties and on call in case of enemy attack. It seemed like a workable way to share the responsibilities associated with being a combat advisor to the ARVNs.

My partner, Slater and I would accompany a company of ARVN Infantry on search & destroy and ambush missions that lasted from 1 to 2 weeks each mission. Our job was to beat the bush with the ARVNs and if we came up against overwhelming enemy fire power we would call for fire support as needed; Gun Ships, Fighter Bombers, Artillery, and twice, B-52s when in Cambodia. While out on the search and destroy missions each day, near dusk, we would set up ambush positions in an effort to catch enemy troops moving through our area of operation (AO). Sometimes the enemy would be moving weapons and munitions to be hidden and stockpiled in underground bunkers that were sometimes concealed beneath homes in area villages or in heavily foliated areas, jungles and bamboo thickets.

COMBINED OPERATIONS

ARVN Troops working with U.S. Troops – We were heading out on a search and destroy mission accompanied by elements of a U.S. Army 25th Infantry Division (Tropic Lightening) mechanized battalion teamed with us, a company of 25th ARVN Infantry Division soldiers in a large-scale operation near the Ho Bo Woods.

The two-day combined mission took place east of the village of Trung Lap in the 25th ARVN area of operations. Intelligence reports categorize this area as a heavy point of infiltration and a staging area for Viet Cong guerilla fighters. Well, we already knew that for it was in our back yard, so to speak and we had been in and around the Ho Bo Woods many times.

Just after dawn, the U.S. troops linked up with us and our ARVN troops at our previous night ambush position. After a brief review of intelligence reports and the plan of action we all went on, under the direction of ARVN company commander Dai Uy (Captain) Trang, to the area to be searched. At this point Sgt. Slater and I had been out with the ARVNs on search and destroy missions for almost two weeks.

This operation was supposed to be a part of the goal to "Vietnamize", gradual transfer of responsibility to the ARVNs. Instead, it only hardened opinions of one another and might I add, it was a very scary moment for me.

I had experienced popping an ambush on U.S. troops before. It happened when a U.S. combat unit had, without prior approval to do so, entered our area of operations on a mission. We had set up night ambush positions and the U.S., unknowingly, walked right into our positions and our guys began shooting thinking they were engaging enemy insurgents. Well, all hell broke loose, star-burst flares, night illumination flares everywhere, and red tracer bullets flying in every direction. U.S. troops were known for over-kill! You don't need napalm and 50 calibers to exterminate an ant hill.

We quickly recognized a bad situation. I grabbed the radio and called headquarters for intervention to get the firefight turned it off as quickly as possible. The U.S. troops ceased fire, but not before there were casualties on both sides.

This combined operation, which had turned into a semi stand-off on the road to the Ho Bo Woods, had nearly become one of those situations.

When we reached the designated area to begin the rift, the tracks went in first and then Slater and I followed along with the ARVN foot soldiers to thoroughly searching the area.

It wasn't long before the ARVNs were uncovering freshly dug tunnels and fighting positions with heavy overhead cover. It was readily apparent to us that the enemy had been there only hours before.

In an effort to avoid casualties from enemy mines and booby-traps that might have been left behind we called in extensive volleys artillery to prep certain areas most suspect.

Judging from the number of secondary explosions set off by the artillery, we might have taken substantial casualties had we not saturated the area first. Even so we suffered one tank disabled after running onto a land mine, fortunately there were no casualties. I had at the time been onto of that tank with some U.S. soldiers. Two of them were dusted-off with bleeding ears, probably punctured ear drums. I suffered the same but was too dumb to request a dust-off for myself, that's another story I won't get into.

With the operation in its final day we netted a large assortment of ammunition, a large stockpile of SKS rifles, AK-47s, and RPG rocket launchers, all wrapped in cosmoline saturated cloth, miscellaneous materials for booby-traps, many large bags of rice 80 lbs. or more, and an assortment of papers, plans and maps..

We also found two men; they were hiding in one of the many tunnels uncovered by the ARVN tunnel rats. The tunnel rats were usually Chu Hoi scouts, former NVA or Viet Cong soldiers who had gone through a repatriation process and been assigned to an ARVN unit to help with locating enemy infiltration zones and their training and staging areas. After preliminary questioning, the men were evacuated by helicopter to an area where they could be more thoroughly interrogated.

With the mission completed the U.S. commanding office expressed his appreciation, it was obvious that he had difficulty doing so. Was this all about building the ARVNs up or tearing them down. My negative opinion of our U.S. combat troops was even more solidified after this experience. My guys were a fine bunch and they demonstrated their bravery and commitment day in and day out on the battle field. I was happy to serve with them and proud to call them my friends.

FREEZE FRAME….. My three-year-old son Gary is turning out to be quite an engineer. He loves to figure out how things work and he loves to build things. One time when we were visiting Grandma and Grandpa, he was playing with Lego building blocks. He had built a couple of forts in the middle of their living room floor. He was happily playing with the forts with his little car and little guy figures. Later I noticed that he had stopped playing and he was just lying on his tummy with his head cradled in his hands, studying the pictures on the Lego container. When his Grandpa asked him what he was doing just staring at that container, he said, "There are some pieces missing here." And he began to point out exactly what pieces were pictured on the box but missing in front of him.

Every once in a while we hit a point in our lives when we stop building long enough to realize that something is missing, something is keeping us from feeling complete. We spend a great deal of our lives so focused on bettering our socioeconomic position in the world that we seem to be missing the meaning of it all. We are suddenly asking ourselves, "What is the purpose of it all, why am I here?"

I have heard it said that we are born with a hole in our heart.... it is a virtual hole and we can never find enough love, enough knowledge, enough whatever to fill that hole in our heart. It is at that moment that we stop and back off from the distractions of life and we focus in the bigger picture. It is in that moment that we discover what really matters and what does not.

It happened some years back to me. I was caught the downsizing of a major corporation. I was walked to the door, laid-off from my job of more than 27 years. I was crushed that my career with this company came down to nothing more than the stroke of a pen.... The letter wished me well and thanked me for my years of dedicated service. After spending a considerable amount of time wallowing in my sorrow over the loss, I turned to God and asked Him, not for a job but to show me what He wanted me to learn from the experience, the loss that I felt. I felt almost as if someone near and dear to me had died, I was grieving over the loss.

At the moment I was seeing very clearly, and seeing that a lot of what our life is about doesn't really matter. Jesus told us what does matter in one of His ultimate values-clarifying statements. It's in Matthew 5: 6., He said: *"Blessed are those who hunger and thirst for righteousness, for they will be filled."* Jesus says that what matters is what happens to your soul.

Deep in the soul of every man, woman, and child is a void that nags us for attention. We think it's a sign of dysfunction, and we try to heal it ourselves. Some of us fill it with food, but the sense of taste is only satisfied for a moment. Some of us fill it with moving from job to job, place to place or possession to possession, but the sense of adventure constantly craves a new direction. Some of us try to fill it with relationships, but another person cannot lastingly fill that void. If we cannot fill it we try to deny it; if we cannot deny it we try to change it and the scenario goes on and on until that one day that we understand that it is a Holy hunger that we suffer from and that the God shaped hole in our heart can only be filled by the Father. Only God can fix it.

Is it about building up or tearing down? It is about establishing and building up our relationship with Jesus and about tearing down the walls we have built up in our lives that keep us from our true destiny which is preparing ourselves for eternity, the life hereafter.

Those feelings that "something is missing" inside are echoes of the emptiness in your soul. And if we don't stop and, as the Bible says, "prepare to meet your God" (Amos 4:12), we will lose our soul forever. The pursuit of this world - its relationships, its accomplishments, and its stuff - can cost you your eternal soul. You can be so busy with earth that you miss heaven - forever.

The most important stop you'll ever make in your life is at the cross of Jesus Christ, where He died to literally save your soul from the punishment for your sins. Ultimately, your God is the missing piece in your life. And the only way to Him is through His Son, the One He sent to die for you. Maybe you've been too busy for Jesus. Then you're fatally busy. God has tapped you on the shoulder today to say, "Stop and take care of your soul, while there's time." You can finally make things right with God. You can have every wrong thing you've ever done forgiven, if you'll reach for Jesus and tell Him today that you're putting all your trust in Him....... Think about it!

Chapter 4
The Waiting Game

The call to pack-up and be prepared for mobilization came late in the evening. It was one of those rare occasions when the whole team was at the base camp and in our house. We had been out that day visiting a nearby U.S. Army artillery base. We were doing our usual bartering, trading captured war souvenirs for building materials, furniture, or food. That particular day we had scored a 5kVa generator to replace our 2.5kVa generator, which was beginning to become overly taxed due to our adding of gadgets, such as a television and some high powered communications equipment in our TOC... that and the continuous parasites bleeding electricity from the main power cable that ran from the generator shed to our hooch. The families of the ARVN soldiers lived with them on our base camp. They had no power to their bunkers and the small buildings they lived in. In the evening they lit their little homes with kerosene lanterns and they cooked on kerosene or wood stoves. In order to steal a bit of electricity they would attach pins or needles to wires and they would pierce the protective housing/insulation of the power cable that connected our house to the generator. The wires attached to the pins and needles led to their homes and provided them a small amount of power, enough to light a bare light bulb or two and power for their radios. Periodically we would take turns at inspecting the power cable, cutting wires and removing pins that connected the power thieves who were draining our power. The battle with the power thieves was minor nuisance and a never ending struggle.

This sort of reminds me of the many power drainers we face in our everyday lives, things that can draw us off course. Just like we had to inspect the cable that delivered power from our generator, likewise we need to continually take inventory of our lives and remove those things that distract us from the things that are really important in our lives; things that are important to our well-being as well as the happiness and security of those who depend on us.

Take addictions, for instance. Are you saying to yourself as you read this, "I am not addicted to anything?" When we think of addictions we automatically think of something dark and sinister; perhaps drug addiction or alcohol. There are many kinds of addictions, too many for me to try to list them here. If we are trying to break simple addictions or very complex addictions the first question we need to ask ourselves is, what is my motivation to remove a power drain from my life?

HURRY UP AND WAIT

In Mid-April, 1970 we received word that our entire battalion was going to redeploy. Our compound would be occupied, and defended by ARVN Regional Forces (RFs). Our orders directed us to make preparations to mobilize ASAP! Where were we being redeployed to? What was the purpose behind the redeployment? What about our house?

Our beloved house that we worked so very hard to build, were we just supposed to leave it behind and entrust is to a group of total strangers? There was a part of our very being in that house. We fought hard and worked hard to build a safe and comfortable place to live, a place that even the rats had a hard time infiltrating. It wasn't glamorous but it was our home and it sure beat living like a rat in a sandbagged bunker, which is what our accommodations would have been, had we not taken on the monumental task of building our house, which was our shelter and sanctuary.

At this point there were many questions but no answers. Two days later we received our answers.

Our orders said we were to redeploy to Tay Ninh City. There was no base camp for us to redeploy to, were we to be a roving band of Nomads? We had spent two days packing up our belongings and supplies, only those that were deemed necessary for defending ourselves and making war on our enemy would accompany us. I hated it, I had to leave behind personal items that were now secured in my footlocker, and at least I hoped they were secured. The only personal items I took with me were my camera and some film, my pocket Bible, given to me by the Gideon's, and my only picture of my son Gary Michael, born just a couple of weeks ago, April 13th. It was his "new born" picture the only one I had received up to this point. Would I ever get to actually see him and hold him? Deep down inside I feared that I would never see him. Would he be shown pictures and told stories about his dad, the man he would never know?

Now we were about to depart this place that had become our home, our sanctuary. Our base camp and our hooch were a place of refuge for us when we returned time after time from beating the bushes on the never-ending pursuit of Charlie. After a quick and unceremonious handing over of the keys to our castle we were off to our destination with no clue of exactly what lie ahead of us. We were band of "armed to the teeth" nomads, scrambling and moving all our troops, provisions, ammunition, and hardware to Tay Ninh City.

TASK FORCE 225 — IN THE SHADOW OF THE BLACK VIRGIN

Hours later our convoy arrived in Tay Ninh City. It was near dusk so we quickly we set up a staging area and bivwak sites and just sat and waited for further orders. I learned in one of our powwows with the military brass that we would be attached to an ARVN Mechanized Infantry Battalion. We would be a combined force of one battalion of foot soldiers and half a battalion of tankers. We were a fighting machine of about 2000 grunts, foot soldiers and tankers.

We anticipated the next move, which would be to invade Cambodia and engage the enemy troops who had been using neighboring Cambodia as a training and staging area. We all knew that there was a stronghold of thousands to tens of thousands of Viet Cong, PAVN, and NVA troops awaiting us on the other side of the border. What we did not know was whether or not we would be engaging an overwhelming force. We did not know if the superior firepower we were comfortably accustomed to would be enough to overwhelm our enemy. We continued to wait….. we continued to wonder if we would come out of this impending invasion alive.

What we did know is that each hour that passed by with us sitting and waiting was another hour for our enemy to plan and size us up. Since they could blend in with the citizens of Tay Ninh, they could gather valuable and accurate intelligence on their opponent… not a good situation. Who the heck developed this strategy of insanity? Days passed, we continued to wait.

JOURNEY INTO THE UNKNOWN

Finally, on April 29, 1970 we received orders to move out. We learned that our combat unit would be known as Task Force 225 and we were to be a part of an invading force known to our ARVN counterparts as Operation TOAN THANG 42. We crossed the border into Cambodia, a territory unknown to us. In the past we had engaged the enemy near the border. Our fire fight would occasionally require us the chase the Viet Cong as they retreated across the border between Vietnam and Cambodia. We had virtually no solid intelligence other than we "might" meet with strong resistance from hard-core NVA regulars. Now that was a comforting thought.

I do not remember what ARVN Mechanized Infantry unit, battalion, or even the regiment that we teamed up with but, we became as one quickly. I will, however, never forget the soldiers I served with during our involvement in the invasion of Cambodia.

After we crossed the border near Tay Ninh City and into Cambodia we advanced with squads of foot soldiers walking point. Almost immediately they established contact with the enemy, coming under fire from small groups of rag-tag armed children who were left behind to inflict as many casualties as they could before becoming casualties themselves, sad, very sad.

After days of minor skirmishes with disjointed, left-behind squads of NVA soldiers we would run across an occasional sniper who would pick off a few of our troops before they were eliminated. Many times the sniper was a teenage boy or girl, tied securely, high up in trees. They were tied to the trees not for their safety, but as an insurance that they would not run and hide, after their comrades had left them behind to slow us down. These children, boys and girls, were considered to be nothing more than a throw-away to the cadre that had abandoned them to a sentence of certain death. The unfortunate children and sometimes women snipers were left behind to slow us down. They did their jobs valiantly but they received no recognition for their bravery, no honorariums, just a quick death in a hail of bullets from machine gun fire.

We would soon learn that the vague intelligence reports were right on. During day 3 we made contact with an enemy faction. We engage them and rather quickly realized that we had made contact with a sizable and heavily armed unit.

We overcame their heavy resistance and after several hours it appeared that whatever was left of the enemy unit had retreated. It would be next to impossible to follow them for they were expert at stashing their weapons and blending in with the occupants of the surrounding villages. We suffered surprisingly light casualties but we had inflicted heavy casualties on the enemy and captured a few dozen prisoners. We found caches of weapons but there were surprisingly few rounds of ammunition. Based on the ferocity of the fire-fight we would have expected heavy stores of ammo and weapons. Another thing peculiar was there were no heavy machine guns and no belt-fed ammo. There were no rockets and launchers. We suspected the resistance we had encountered was yet another smoke screen force left behind to slow us down.

As we pushed on further into Cambodia we continued to experienced fairly light and sporadic enemy contact. We found many more abandoned makeshift villages that appeared to be staging and training areas for the NVA and Viet Cong. They were strewn with large bags of rice, cooking utensils and water jugs, but again, there was no evidence of weaponry left behind or destroyed during a hasty retreat.

We were now moving into an area about 20 km west of Svay Rieng. We are passing by a small village, the people of the village are moving toward the road to greet us. These people were really the first natives of Cambodia that we've seen. I notice that their features are slightly different from the average Vietnamese people I'd been accustomed to seeing. The Cambodian villagers were darker skinned than the Vietnamese and their eyes are slightly rounder. Their hair was thick and black and wavy to curly. Many of the young women were wearing sarongs and were topless, bare breasted. I later learned that the young, unmarried and young childless women normally do not cover their breasts, not that is valuable information or critical to our mission, just an observation that was hard to overlook, having been away from my home in the U.S. for so long.

As the people get closer to us I notice that they are staring quite intently at me and the other American advisors. As we dismount our tanks and APCs to greet the villagers they immediately move toward us, some of them begin speaking to us in French. Our interpreter tells us that they think we are Frenchmen. Suddenly the people begin to run back to their village. We do not know what the problem is at first, but later we discover that when the villagers realized that we were not Frenchmen but in fact we were American soldiers. They were terrified of us; they thought we might to kill them. They have been propagandized into believing that all Americans are cold-blooded killers.

These people have never seen an American and many of them have never seen a Caucasian person. Once they are convinced by the ARVNs that we are not killers they begin to return. As they stare at us they seem to be fascinated by the color of our eyes and the color of our hair. They offer us fresh water from their wells and even invite us to eat a meal with them, which we happily agree to. The officers and advisors are invited to eat with the village chief and the elders while the others are treated to a meal with the villagers.

After our meal and exchanging of pleasantries the intelligence officers begin to question the village chief and the elders about any activity they have observed or any interaction they may have had with NVA, Viet Cong, or PAVN forces in the recent past. Basically we learn that they have witnessed medium to large groups of soldiers moving toward the west, further toward the interior of Cambodia. As night falls we set up a command post outside the village and prepare for night ambush. Ah….. we experience a restful, uneventful night.

Around May 7th we discovered a cleverly hidden hospital. While searching near a deserted village for hidden bunkers our guys looked into what appeared to be a well. Inside the walls of the well was a wooden bottom that gave the appearance that it was a dry well that had been covered. When wood was removed the ARVNs discovered that is was NOT a dried up well but a concealed bunker or tunnel complex. After some discussion between company commanders and surmising the situation it was decided to investigate rather than destroy the bunker or tunnel complex.

Cautiously one of our Tunnel Rats entered the opening, being careful to look closely for trip wires of possible booby traps. (FYI, a Tunnel Rat is sort of like a special teams football player.) He is a soldier who, armed with a pistol, a grenade or two, and a flashlight, enters bunkers and tunnels and inspects them). After a quick search he came out and excitedly informed the company commander that the underground area was clear of booby traps, but there was another level beneath the one he had just searched. The search was continued by only the one man, the Tunnel Rat. The company commander did not want to risk the lives of additional men, in case there were undiscovered booby traps in the underground structure. Time passed, it seemed like an eternity waiting for the ARVN soldier to emerge or awaiting the unwelcomed explosion of tripped booby traps. Suddenly I heard the excited chatter of the ARVN soldiers surrounding the well. Out of the well came a young woman who appeared to be hysterical and terrified. Then a second and third young woman emerged from the hole in the ground, it appeared that they were all very afraid. The women were quickly turned over to our interrogators in order to gather any possible valuable information from them. After the interrogation we learned that the underground structure was an NVA field hospital complex containing more than 200 beds and an operating room, the three women were nurses.

The well or the hole in the ground, lead into the complex which was a crude three-story underground hospital, constructed of bamboo and timbers. When it was deemed that the underground hospital was cleared of booby traps, I entered with a group of my ARVN counterparts. It was dank and dark; I can still vividly recall the musty, earthy smell. As I looked around I tried to imagine what the area had looked like when the hospital was in service. Had wounded soldiers actually been treated here? If so, how on earth did they ever survive in such crude and unsanitary conditions? After inspecting the first level I exited hospital, which to me appeared to be nothing more than a cave. I am not claustrophobic, but the thought of going down the stairs to the second and third levels was absolutely out of the question for me. I had to get out and into the daylight and fresh air or I felt I might suffocate. I suppose the hospital had served its purpose. Upon further inspection the ARVNs discovered a considerable amount of medical supplies. The medical supplies were removed and relocated to one of our supply vehicles, they would be valuable assets in treating our own wounded, should the need arise. After any items of value were removed C-4 explosive charges were placed throughout the structure, then it was blown, destroyed so that it would be of no further use to the enemy.

DRAWN INTO THE SNARE

The underlying feeling of being "drawn in" rather than being in hot pursuit of our foe would soon become more than just a feeling. The frequent skirmishes should have been the key to the fact that the sly enemy was drawing us into his "spider-web." Their continued retreat following fierce battle was actually a well executed plan. I am sure that the commanders of the enemy troops felt that even though they had sacrificed the lives of relatively high numbers of their soldiers, it was for the good of the whole. Flawed thinking in my opinion, but it made sense that an enemy that fought on against all odds would stop at nothing to achieve the goal of reuniting their country under the communist leadership of Ho Chi Minh.

It was sometime after the 9th of May, we were moving across a flat-land covered with scrub brush. Off in the distance there was a wood line; it appeared to be a heavily forested area. I was atop an APC that was armed with dual-50 caliber machine guns. We had been experiencing an uneasy feeling each day as we moved further into Cambodia. All-in-all we had been fortunate, having suffered only light casualties with relatively few wounded. We enjoyed rather lop-sided victories over our enemy, inflicting numerous KIAs and capturing high numbers of prisoners. Fortunately we had encountered very few mechanical issues and no breakdowns of the tracked vehicles, life seemed to be good, for being in a war-zone, surrounded by people that wanted to kill us. That was all about to change.

On this day, much like our other encounters with the enemy our advance teams walking point had come in contact with what at first appeared to be another moderately sized band of VC. That is the way this fire-fight began. This fire-fight however, was quite different from the previous several days. We soon realized that our opponents were well armed and there appeared to be a significant number of enemy adversaries.

As we moved across the flat-land toward the wood line we were flanked by our ARVN foot-soldiers. Spread out and a bit to our left front were about 200 of our guys and another 200 spread out to our right and slightly in front of us. I was among a core group of APCs and tanks, we were all moving toward the wood line where our guys were engaging enemy soldiers. The ferocity of the fire fight was quickly growing.

Suddenly and without warning in my peripheral vision I saw what appeared to be the ground moving! It took only moments for my mind to process what I was witnessing. Spider holes were popping open, virtually all around us. I watched in horror as all hell broke loose around me and our entire position. It was a surreal experience, one that I will never forget. As if in slow motion I saw figures, camouflaged with foliage, spring up and take aim in all directions. Some held AK-47 automatic rifles, and some had RPG Rocket Launchers. Standing in the holes, each took deadly aim on targets to their front, rear, or either side. AK-47s were spraying a lethal wall of bullets in all directions while the RPG armor piercing rocket grenades were disabling or destroying tanks and armored personnel carriers. As the horrific scene played out all around me our guys began returning fire. I began emptying my M-16 in the direction of any spider hole that I could see. It was almost like being at a shooting gallery, bullets were flying everywhere. I could hear them as they whizzed past me and the "tink-splat-tink" of the bullets as they struck our armored vehicle. The ARVNs that were on the APC with me were firing non-stop in all directions.

The enemy soldiers that were firing from the spider holes were in a hopeless predicament. Basically they were dead men hell-bent to deliver maximum damage and casualty for the higher cause. The only way they were going to come out of those spider holes would be as bullet riddled corpses. There would be no fanfare for them. No one would praise them for their bravery and courage. One by one they were silenced, but not before they had done their merciless deeds.

The element of surprise had worked for them. Several of the APCs and a couple of the tanks were severely damaged and immobilized. The surprise attack had inflicted severe casualties on us, many were killed or wounded. I will never forget the APC drivers and many that were inside of the vehicles; their charred bodies with faces frozen into a twisted, dying grimace. These men, some of them my friends, suffered a death that we cannot even imagine. They lost their lives as a result of a cleverly planned and courageously launched sneak attack.

I looked around quickly to ensure that there were no more manned spider holes. As I surveyed the area I could see black smoke billowing from one of our tanks and a couple of APCs. The air was permeated with the heavy odor of burning oil mixed with the stench of burning flesh. I can still hear the screams of men inside a nearby charred APC. It had a gaping hole near the front of the tracked vehicle. I could see the driver's burnt remains hanging out of the hatch at the front of the APC. Foot soldiers were frantically trying to get the back door of the vehicle open to get to the wounded still trapped inside. As I was observing all that was going on around me I became aware of the pop, pop, pop of machine gun fire... it appeared to be coming from the wood line in front of us. I could actually hear the zip sound of an occasional bullet as it whizzed by. I should have been paralyzed with fear, but instead I turned sideways to the direction of the wood line. It was a sort of involuntary defensive move so as to not provide as large a target as I was when directly facing the enemy positions.

I could see more of our units advancing and taking cover. The APC I was riding on appeared to have come out of the mêlée unscathed. Abruptly it jerked into action, racing forward and to the side for the cover of some nearby trees. As the ARVN commanders were quickly assessing the situation and developing a plan of action the 50-caliber machine guns and probably every M-16 rifle and every M-79 grenade launcher was firing a hail of bullets and explosives at the wood line.

This fire-fight had started as no other had since we had crossed the border between Cambodia and Vietnam. Some of the previous fire-fights were intense but the increasing fire power coming from this wood line was fierce and unrelenting. It seemed as if rifle fire was coming from every tree in the wood line. I could hear the mounting bursts of heavy machine gun fire, probably Soviet 51 caliber guns. In our skirmishes since crossing the border, we had not come up against any heavy caliber weapons and any RPGs or mortar fire. The bad guys were probably saving all of that for this very moment. Did they plan to overwhelm and overtake us? Perhaps this was their stand-off, a do-or-die assignment from their higher command. Whatever it was they were fighting with all tenacity that could be expected of them. Could we match their game and over take them? We were operating on intelligence, they however, had the advantage of knowing the enemy units they were fighting against... after all, our two or three delay in invading their strong-holds gave them the advantage of sizing us up before we made our move.

I could see some of our armored units breaking off to the left and to the right; it appeared they were going to attempt to flank the enemy, still unseen in the wood line. As the flanking maneuvers were taking place I could tell that the intensity of gunfire and explosions had increased and expanded. The enemy had anticipated and prepared with counter maneuvers. I learned that intelligence believed that we were up against an enemy force that was comprised of portions of several NVA and PAVN fighting units. We were possibly engaged with battalions of the 7th and 9th NVA divisions and at least 3 companies of PAVN units.

This fire-fight seemed to be with a much more formidable opponent than we had faced in Cambodia and perhaps even in Vietnam. Quickly doing the math in my head it was apparent that we were definitely outnumbered by our enemy. We could only hang on to the hope that we would outgun them and overwhelm them with our fire power, which had been superior to the enemy's fire power in each and every combat action I had been involved in… thus far.

I had a sickening feeling in my stomach. It felt like I had swallowed a rock. We had been lured into exactly the place where our challengers had planned. What else did they have up their sleeves? Surely with our fire power we could overwhelm them… couldn't we? All contacts with the enemy had gone our way. Even though there were some close calls, we had prevailed. If our latest intelligence reports had been accurate, we were up against a formidable opponent with overwhelming man-power. If they decided to make a death charge toward us could they overrun our positions? Only time would tell and I needed to get those thoughts out of my head and concentrate on what was actually taking place. Keep my head clear and ready to call for whatever support was necessary.

In the three days that the fire-fight raged on we suffered heavy casualties. Before it was all over we had called in every type of heavy support at our disposal; numerous volleys artillery delivered by 175 mm. Howitzers and 8-inch guns complements of the U.S. Army artillery. Numerous sorties of high-explosives and napalm bombs delivered by U.S. Air Force F4 and F-111 fighter jets, and even two sorties delivered by B-52 bombers.

Last but not least, after the heavy fire of the enemy had been all but silenced helicopter gunships were called to deliver the coups d'état. If you have never witnessed the firepower of a Cobra gunship it is quite an awesome and sobering site. The gunships, equipped with rockets and mini-guns went to work carpeting the area with heavy mini-gun fire and unleashing sortie after sortie of rocket fire. It seemed as if the gunships were firing needlessly into an area where an already beaten and over killed enemy had nearly overrun our positions.

Incredibly the gunships were drawing intermittent small arms fire. The NVA forces were fierce fighters who would never give up until they had drawn their last breath. They were my enemy, they wanted to kill me, but as I look back today, my hate for them has been replaced by an eerie sort of admiration for their bravery and their dedication to the cause they believed in.

This was a major, major fire-fight. We had engaged an enemy with a tenacity that is matched by few. The enemy had however suffered far greater losses than we. Remnants of the two NVA regiments surrendered or were captured; many more escaped and blended themselves into the surrounding villages.

We were severely fatigued and spirits were low for all of us. We had just undergone days of grueling battle. We had seen the horrors of war; our munitions had been severely depleted. Our troops needed to stand-down and rest, relax, and rearm. There would be rearming, but the rest and relaxation for Task Force 225 would have to be put on hold. We had an unpleasant task ahead of us, one that had to be carried out... body count and completion of after-action reports. Paperwork, paperwork... you can never get around it! But first we had to arrange for the mass evacuation of our wounded and dead. We had to interrogate our prisoners and evacuate them also. Some of them would be kept with us to be used as scouts, assisting us in finding weapons caches and ferreting out their comrades who had blended in or retreated.

Body count.... an awful process but it was one that had to be done. The top brass wanted to quantify success or failure; this was the only way to satisfy that need. I learned early on in my career as a combat advisor, the smell of death is something that you will never, ever forget. My first team leader in Vietnam had told me that I should keep a couple of cigars in my pocket. They would come in handy on just such an occasion. The over-powering fragrance of the cigar helps to mask the stench of death. In my mind I said, "Thank you Đại Úy".... then I lit a cigar....

The remainder of that day and part of the next were consumed with body count and after-action reports. Also there was an abundance of Army brass, U.S. as well as ARVN, wanting to touch down in the area for their photo-ops and an opportunity for check marks toward their Air Combat Assault Ribbons. This fire-fight occurred somewhere West of Svay Rieng, Cambodia.

Many of our men died, some were friends and some were only acquaintances, I soldiered with them; I drank beers (Ba Moui Ba, beer 33, AKA "Tiger Piss") with them in the Cau Lac Bo. I was an amateur body builder at one time, I guess that's why they always wanted to arm wrestle me. We had a good time together. Even though we did not often hang out together we were comrades. When in the field we watched each other's back. I am sure that I owe my life to at least some of them.

Chapter 5
Never Go Back the Way You Came

Never go back the way you came... this is something I learned quickly as a soldier and I remember it to this day. The experience of combat strangely parallels this phrase I once wrote a long time ago. I do not know if it was an original thought... perhaps it was something I heard or read somewhere. Never the less it has a profound meaning, both in war and in everyday life. Let me explain:

Vietnam was an indescribable place in the reality of my world back in 1970 and it is not a stretch to say, it was not on the map of the conscious mind of most green soldiers of that time. They were mostly inexperienced in the realities of war, new arrivals to Southeast Asia. The nightmare of war, however, quickly became reality for the combat soldier, an experience that would never really be forgotten. My chest tightens as I write this, even these many years later.

To this day it remains a ghostly and surreal experience to me. Today I only read the news or see the happenings of war on TV. The difference is, today every now and then when I go to sleep at night; I have dreams of being in combat again. I see myself taking cover in a bamboo thicket, calling in helicopter gunships with their mini-guns blazing, delivering more than 1000 rounds per minute and rockets zipping through the sky with expert and deadly accuracy toward their intended target. In dreams I sometimes experience the sights, sounds, and even the smells of an air strike I had called in to blast our enemy into submission or complete annihilation.

I can still see it as if it were just yesterday. The U.S. Air Force, Forward Air Controller (FAC) approaches our area in a single engine, fixed wing airplane. I think to myself that he is more vulnerable to enemy fire than I am, but still he goes about his task in a professional and expert manner. He identifies himself over the radio with his code name, I immediately answer with my code name. Next he responds, "Pop smoke" (pop smoke means to release a smoke grenade to mark our ground position so the FAC can verify there to be no friendly's within the impact zone of the bombs.) After marking of our troop location with a colored smoke grenade, the FAC identifies the color of our smoke grenade marker in a playful way describing the colors as "goofy grape" or "lemon yellow."

Next the FAC responds, "Hang tight gentlemen, sit back, relax, and enjoy the air show. Let the fireworks begin." Suddenly off in the distance I can hear the roar of the approaching fighter jets. Instantly they begin to dive, delivering sortie after sortie of high explosives bombs in an effort to blast the enemy into submission or oblivion. In either case it is a powerful and fearful demonstration of our superior fire-power. I think to myself that I am so thankful that I don't have to face an enemy with fire-power that even equals ours. Our enemy's strength often lies in the element of surprise, not to mention the incredible tenacity and dedication to their cause.

Once the adversary appears to be stunned from the bombardment, the fighter jets might release a salvo of dozens of rounds from their 20 mm. canons to finish any remaining fight left in the bad guys. Once the fighter jets have finished their handy work the FAC radio back and ask for us to be sure to post a body count that resulted from the air assault. We exchange a few pleasantries and FAC departs the area. Over and hopefully done with, or is it? Next a company of ARVNs splits to flank the area, we cautiously approach behind them. Suddenly there are short bursts of fire from AK-47s and I hear the familiar sound of RPGs coming our way. Badly wounded and perhaps even dying the enemy still fights back.

In some fire-fights the jets would deliver napalm bombs on the targets. Napalm unleashes an incredible and indiscriminant river of fire, which strikes terror in the hearts of the enemy and sadly often in hearts of the villagers, the farmers and their families who were being held by the enemy as human shields. These unfortunate and innocent people are reduced to nothing more than collateral damage. They are an unpleasant but all too real cost of conducting the dirty business or war.

No one in the vicinity of the napalm survives and often times there are no traces of the victims of the river of fire. All that remains are ashes of what may have once been a peaceful and bustling small rural village. Once again I can see myself in dreams working with my ARVN counterparts as we go through the grizzly tasks necessary to record enemy body count for our military intelligence group.

Our life experiences become a part of us; they remain in our sub-conscious. I suppose once having been there, in combat, you can never really leave it behind. The experiences remain a part of our subliminal being.

During the war I wrote in a letter to home, "Once you travel through the door of an experience, you can never go back the way you came." In other words, you can recover from calamity but you will remain changed by it forever. I don't mean for that statement to sound negative, on the contrary, if we do not allow ourselves to be consumed by the blunt force of combat or by any other of life's tragedies, we will experience a strengthening, a tempering, we will be more capable of coping and we will move on with life rather than being trapped by our experience. Perhaps we might even be able to help others as they wrestle with the aftermaths of disaster, misfortune, or heartbreaking loss.

I submit to you that I may have never been able to cope with these experiences without my faith. My faith sustained me through it all. The knowledge that God was with me then and to this day He is still with me. God has a purpose for my life and He has purpose for your life too.

Are you one of the broken? There is hope for you.

Are you struggling in understanding one of the broken? There is hope for you. Jesus said, "Come to me, all who are broken and weary and I will give you rest."

OUT OF TOUCH

I served alongside the ARVN soldiers. Day in, day out I humped the countryside with them. I ate with them, bathed in the same bomb craters as they did. We picked leaches and fire ants off one another. I fought the enemy with them, shoulder to shoulder on many combat missions. They were my comrades and many of them became my friends. Sadly, many times I saw my friends die and as I prayed for them and their families, I could not help but wonder why I had survived the fire-fight that had taken their lives. I've spoken with veterans of combat and some of them express to me that they sometimes feel guilty that their friends perished and they made it out alive. I'm here to tell you that there is no shame in surviving. The baggage of guilt can be a heavy and overwhelming load to bear. There is hope for us, the survivors, if only we can find the strength to give it to the One for whom no load is too heavy to bear.

Most of my other contacts with the people of Vietnam involved meeting villagers in rice paddies as the planted or tended their rice. They would stare at me with suspicion in their eyes. Their misgivings of the "round eyes" American soldiers, was well founded. These people had suffered through years of abuse from "Charlie", the Viet Cong guerillas, and from the communist backed North Vietnamese Army (NVA). They had been beaten and interrogated by their own countrymen, my comrades the ARVNs. They had to stand by while soldiers of the U.S. Army or ROK Marines burned their villages and killed their livestock. We were not all the great, liberating American soldiers. Some American soldiers harassed the villagers, treating them like second class citizens, calling them "slope heads" or "gukes." Believe me, I witnessed the harassment but, was helpless to prevent it... don't make waves.

Sometimes I would have to act as a negotiator, a spokesman for my government, attempting to pacify a farmer whose water buffalo we had accidentally killed during a fire-fight with Viet Cong guerillas. After a brief parley and reaching a deal on the value of his animal, I would radio in a request for monetary compensation to the farmer. The farmer was seldom satisfied with the negotiated amount but none the less would hesitantly accept it as compensation.

On more than one occasion my partner and I spent a few hours making personal contact with the inhabitants of a friendly village while we and our ARVN counterparts were searching their homes and the village area. The searches were initiated mainly as a deterrent for villagers to hide Viet Cong soldiers or caches of enemy weapons and supplies in concealed bunkers beneath their homes.

At times the searches were instigated by intelligence reports, hastily compiled and based on sometimes outdated or otherwise flawed information. On those occasions where we received inaccurate information, the experience was, let's say not gratifying for the villagers who would be grilled by interrogators trying to pry information from an unfortunate villager or two who had no clue as to what the interrogators were pressing them for. Sometimes the villagers would be taken into custody and moved to another location for further interrogation.

In short the villagers and farmers just wanted to be left alone to live in peace. In their reality it mattered little whether or not they lived in a democracy or under communism. Their lot in life would still be hard work each day just to get by, just to be able to feed their family and live a simple life.

LOOKS ARE DECEIVING — PERCEPTIONS ARE MISLEADING

The perception of the "real" Vietnamese people shared by most of the tens of thousands of U.S. personnel working out of air-conditioned buildings in Saigon, Bien Hoa, and other major U.S. installations was a large-scale version of the Tu Do Street Bar Girls, the Boom-Boom Girls as they were called, and the Hooch Bas they came in contact with. The Hooch Ba is a woman that cleans barracks and hooches and does laundry for the U.S. soldiers. As for the Boom-Boom girls, I will let your imagination paint that picture for you. My teammates and I were among the virtual handful of Covan My (U.S. Advisors) and Special Forces who were the only American citizens actually living among the Vietnamese as opposed to being geographically within Vietnam.

My teammates and I were not isolated from the real local people, but we were definitely isolated from reality, as we had known it before being TAKEN away. This surrealistic world, into which we had been thrust, soon became *our* reality. While out on search and destroy missions or any combat mission, for that matter, you must change your location frequently else the enemy will sneak up on you and then you are GONE.

On one such mission while our unit was on deployment in Cambodia we had been moving further into the country. After a major, major battle mentioned in chapter 4 we had again been engaging in minor skirmishes over the period of several days. As I had mentioned also before silencing the enemy in that major battle, an undetermined number of them had escaped. They had decided to cut and run to fight another day. They had, for all intents and purposed, blended in with the general population. More than likely they had been closely watching us, maybe even smiling and waving to us as we passed by villages and villagers along the roads. That was an eerie feeling for me, knowing that eyes were always upon you. Many of them hated you and wanted to kill you, while to others you represented something that they just wished would go away so they could live in peace.

On this particular day, we had moved our location about 30 kilometers. We were in the process of setting up our Command Post (CP). We had come upon a Buddhist temple located in a semi-jungle setting. I do not recall exactly where this Buddhist temple was in relation to a major city, but it reminded me of a movie set you'd see in an Indiana Jones episode. The temple was located a just few kilometers from a nearby village. It just reminded me of a picturesque setting you'd see in a travelogue or on a picture post card. Here was this rather large temple, set back into a heavily forested area. Vines and moss, all the movie props were there. As we were in the process of establishing our CP and squads were being deployed to set up a perimeter; we were greeted by a group of seemingly friendly Buddhist Monks. This group of men was dressed in the orange robe uniform we had become so accustomed to seeing the monks attired in. Their shaved heads and smiling faces hid a plan, a sinister plot that only they were aware of.

The monks invited to enter the temple to see its beauty. They were all smiling and bowing, greeting us as we approached the doorway of the temple. After removing our shoes, as was the custom, we entered the temple. The beauty of its ornate decorations was almost indescribable. The floor was covered ceramic tiles arranged in intricate and ornate designs. The walls were painted with very elaborate patterns with dragons like figures intermingled at intervals throughout the designs. There were beautiful silk hangings in many places throughout the large room. At the back wall of the temple was a gigantic statue of Buda. It was a very beautiful and memorable place... I will never forget the experience that would soon become forever etched in my mind.

We finished setting up our CP very near the temple and our perimeter squads were in place before sunset. The squads were entrenched to guard against attack and ready to ambush any attempted enemy incursion. That night we were hit, it was an unexpected double whammy. Suddenly we heard the not too distant staccato of machine gun fire and explosions, our squads on the outposts were under attack. Unexpectedly, out of the darkness came machine gun fire at close range. I actually could see the fire from the mussel blast; our CP was under attack as well. How did the enemy break through our perimeter so quickly? Who could it be? Fortunately the firefight within our midst ended rather quickly. We later learned that our attackers came from inside the temple and many of them were soldiers disguised as Buddhist Monks or so we surmised and others were uniformed NVA soldiers that must have been hidden in the catacombs beneath the temple. Fortunately, we suffered few casualties and many of the enemy posing as monks were captured. Our interrogators were able to extract from those captured, much valuable information. The group that had attacked us were a part of the units we had the major battle with days earlier. I don't recall that we ever learned what might have happened to the real Buddhist monks.

I'll never forget the way I felt that night, violence and mayhem exploding all around me in the darkness. We had little time to react and take defensive positions. I commend my ARVN comrades for maintaining a semblance of order in the midst of total chaos. The outcome of this event could have had a very different ending. Sporadic machine gun continued through the night and there were a few poorly aimed mortar explosions. It was a very long night, I am sure we all felt the effects of sleep deprivation, but as daylight broke the loss of sleep quickly disappeared. The enemy sent out a wave of soldiers, they made a death charge in an attempt to overrun our outpost squads. Fortunately our guys valiantly fought them off, inflicting numerous casualties on the would-be intruders.

While this all was going on we had sent a squad in to make sure the temple was cleared of any danger it could impose on us. The inspection yielded several crates of Russian made SKS rifles, a few cases of RPG grenades and launchers, and other miscellaneous weapons and explosives. As one would expect of our adversaries, they had booby trapped the entrance to the underground catacombs, but our guys discovered the trip wires and disarmed the explosive devices before they could cause any casualties.

We broke camp and started advancing toward the area where the attacks had come from. We left units to our rear to prevent another sneak attack from Charlie at our back door. We were moving in a direction toward the nearby village. This was not a good situation for our enemy was well known for hiding in villages, using the inhabitants as a shield. They were relying on the humanity of their enemy. Our worst suspicions would come true; the bad guys were firing at our positions from within and around the village. Our ARVN commanders wanted to hold off on an all out attack on the village in hopes that we might wear the enemy down or run them low enough on ammunition that they might withdraw from the village. The safety of the villagers was a concern that our foe had counted on.

Our rifleman held their positions, returning fire to positions where they could spot muzzle blast or actually see the shooter. The exchange of fire continued until late in the day. There were intermittent mortar attacks on our positions and for the most part their aim was poor although some of the mortar rounds came dangerously close a few times. As daylight dwindled, suddenly we heard a heavy concentrated machine gun fire coming from a wooded area near the outskirts of the village. We saw people running from the wood line; they appeared to be villagers attempting to escape. Our commander told our troops to hold fire, not to shoot at the running people. Sadly none of them made good their escape. The enemy, NVA or VC had shot the running people in the backs to prevent them from escaping. Our adversaries were cold hearted killers and they had to be stopped. The anger within me began to build and build. We could not risk sending our guys out to see if any of the people attempting to escape was still alive… not a good situation.

That night, again, there was intermittent rifle and machine gun fire and the lobbing of mortar rounds. A squad on our outer perimeter reported that they encountered and captured several people who had escaped from the village; they were bringing them toward the CP. Our commander ordered them to stop and thoroughly search each of the people before bringing them any closer to our position. They needed to ensure that none of the escapees were carrying explosives or weapons. It was not unheard of for enemy soldiers to disguise themselves as friendly's and walk right in and blow themselves up in your midst. Once they were all searched and cleared they were brought to us for questioning and interrogation, again to ensure that they were in fact villagers and not enemy defectors.

Daylight came and more of the same, more sporadic fire in both directions, some helicopter fly-over's in attempts to surmise what we were up against. Our commander decided to take a more aggressive approach sending some tanks toward the village and the wood lines. The tanks delivered several cannon volleys and machine gun fire. He sent a Zippo (flame thrower tank) up to set the wood line on fire. This maneuver brought on more rifle and machine gun fire. We noticed in the wood line beyond the area that had been set on fire, there was a large group of people gathered at the edge of the cleared field. Suddenly they broke into an all out run, spreading out and running for their very lives, running toward our location. I could see that among them were women carrying small children. Gunfire broke out; the enemy was shooting at the people who were trying to escape. The ARVNs returned heavy volleys of fire to try to silence the riflemen shooting at the villagers who were running toward us. Some of the villagers fell but most of them made it to cover near us. A tank was sent out to shield the villagers, it protected them and guided them to a secure area where they could be safely searched and questioned.

The escapee villagers were kept in a safe place but at a distance from our CP. There was an old woman holding a baby, the old lady was crying hysterically and appeared to be asking for help. An ARVN medic responded to the old woman's cries for help. I could see that he took the baby from the woman's arms and he appeared to be working on the baby. I made my way over to where they were and I saw that the medic was treating an abdominal wound that the baby had suffered, probably while they were escaping, running for their lives. What I was witnessing was very troubling to me and at the same time very touching. Just a month before my son Gary Michael was born, I had never seen my son. I carried with me the only picture I had, his new born photograph. I felt as if this were my Gary Michael and if it were, I would want the medic to do all he possibly could to save him.

I watched as the medic treated the baby and wrapped the wound. It appeared that a bullet had struck the little guy in the stomach and passed through and exited his back, below his rib cage. No telling what damage had been done internally. The medic attempted to give the baby back to the old woman but she was not going to take the baby back. I gathered by the conversation that the baby did not belong to her and she wanted the medic to keep the baby with him. I stepped in and offered to take the baby. I took the baby boy and cradled him in my arms; he appeared to be about one year old, perhaps a couple months older. His age was not my concern, but his welfare was of extreme importance to me. I carried him back to an area that was shaded by a camouflaged canopy. I sat on the rear hatch of an APC and held the little guy and tried my best to comfort him. He didn't fuss at all, just laid listlessly in my arms, occasionally gasping for air. It was all I could do to keep from crying.

As I held the baby and prayed rocked him in my arms I looked out at the group of villagers as they sat on the edge of a rice paddy. Some of them were looking back, watching me rock the baby. Their faces were expressionless. What were they thinking as they watched me… I will never know. I hope they realized that I cared for the little boy, even though I did not know him, even though I was an unwelcomed soldier from a far away land. I hope they knew that I felt love and a deep concern for the little boy.

Cambodian Villagers Awaiting Evacuation

The fire-fight raged on, it had even kicked up a few notches. I could see the medic treating some of the escaped villagers as they sat on the edge of the rice paddy. A few more villagers had fled to safety since this first bunch had arrived. The people quietly suffered in the hot sun, some of them asking for water. The baby's breathing started to become more labored. I called the medic, but argued that he said he had done all that he could for the baby. What was I to do? I felt that something needed to be done for the baby or surely he would die right there in my arms. My thoughts kept flashing to the picture I held in my pocket, the new born picture of my son Gary Michael, my gut twisted.

GOING AGAINST THE GRAIN

We were under strict orders that while in Cambodia; all dust-offs (medivac helicopter extractions) would be done by ARVN helicopters and personnel. The only dust-offs that would be done by U.S. helicopters would be if there were U.S. personnel down, wounded. We had called for a dust-off to evacuate the wounded villagers and the baby, more than an hour had passed since we radioed the request, still no response, no affirmation that help was on the way. The time passed, the baby's breathing became more labored, and he was now gasping frequently for air and he'd grown pale and listless. I made a decision; I got on the radio and called for a dust-off, "U.S. down." I gave them our grid coordinates, confirmed that there were U.S. wounded and awaiting evacuation to a medical facility.

Soon I heard the familiar whup-whup-whup of a Huey medivac chopper. I felt relief and at the same time I had a sinking feeling in my gut. I knew I was in trouble, but what the heck! The chopper landed nearby in a safe area, I hurried toward the chopper with the baby in my arms and the more severely wounded villagers were helped to the chopper by the ARN medics. The chopper crew stared at us in disbelief, "Where are the wounded U.S.?" they yelled. I explained to them that there had been a miscommunication and that these people were in need of medical attention and the baby was severely wounded, life threatening. They took the baby and loaded the people in, as they were doing so the chopper co-pilot started to argue back again and I said, "I suggest that you get into the air and out of the area, it's not safe." They took off and I... had some "SPLAININ TO DO." I knew there would be repercussions. Believe me, there were!

I was relieved that the baby was whisked off to safety, but I knew his chances of making it through were not good. I prayed for the little guy off and on the rest of that day.

That evening the outposts called back and said they had taken several people into custody, some of them were enemy deserters. The same calls were radioed through the night; more enemy soldiers were defecting and surrendering. Day three rolled around and our battalion commanders decided to flank the area and make an all-out assault on the village. After some intense gun battles, it all ended rather abruptly. Some of the bad guys had retreated, but a good number of them surrendered. Had they run out of ammo or did they have more tricks up their sleeves? No matter, it was over for the moment and surprisingly the villagers that remained had taken cover and they suffered few casualties. Everyone was glad it was over, even the enemy defectors.

The prisoners were herded into a holding area where they were questioned. The ones who had fought and were forced to surrender were kept separate from the Chu Hoi (means "safe passage" for those who surrender voluntarily), those who had voluntarily surrendered. The wounded were moved to yet another area, I never saw any of them again.

Later that afternoon I heard that some top brass was coming to review the battle and discuss tactic employed by the ARVN battalion commanders. This was a customary exercise, to review battle plan tactics that worked and those did not work so well and the counter-measures the enemy had taken. War is a lot like an NFL football game. You have the scouts (intelligence command), battle plans (the play book), counter measures employed (play changes); head coaches (battalion commanders).

I heard the "whup-whup-whup-whup" of approaching helicopters; I could see there were two helicopter gunships, M-60s machine guns hanging out of each side of the choppers. They circled the area a few times and then we heard the approach of the rest of the entourage. Two more helicopters escorted by another two gunships. The helicopters landed except for the first two gunships, which continued to fly large circular patterns around the area to ensure security. Was it time for me to pay the piper?

Our ARVN battalion commanders and Senior Advisor moved toward the choppers to greet the senior field commanders, I could see an ARVN Lt. General accompanied by his team and our MACV Team commander, a full bird Colonel with his team. Out came the maps and "playbooks", their pow-wow lasted for a bit, and then I saw the brass break-out, some of them mingling with the troops and more photo ops. I saw an all too familiar figure approaching me; he was the senior advisor to several teams, a Lt. Colonel who preferred to be addressed as "Reb." He was a hard-nosed, veteran of many battles. He was tough but fair and he garnered the respect of any combat soldier, on his chest he wore the Combat Infantryman's Badge with two stars. The two stars signified that Reb had seen combat in two wars prior to the Vietnam War. Reb had been in combat in WWII where he received a field commission as an officer, and he'd also seen action in Korea. Reb was on his was to see me and I had the sick feeling that I knew why he was headed toward me.

My suspicions were correct; the conversation was completely one-sided; he spoke, I listened. I was laid-out in lavender, the conversation ended with him telling me that under any other circumstances he would see me court-martialed for disobeying a direct order that jeopardized the lives of other U.S. personnel. End of discussion.

Sometimes you just need to go against the grain. In this case, the Lt. Colonel was correct, I disobeyed a direct order and that order was neither illegal nor immoral, therefore I should have, as a soldier under the authority of my superiors, obeyed the order. I chose to preservation of life over a direct order. Having made that choice I did not consider consequences to myself or to others. Reb did not know my motives for choosing to ignore orders. I never explained to him why and I am sure he was not interested why. I am not sorry that I chose to ignore the order and hopefully lives were saved by my decision. On the other hand, if that medivac helicopter had been shot down.......

DON'T MAKE WAVES

Our VIP visitors had unceremoniously departed the area. It was back to the business of war for us. One of the first matters at hand.... search for booby traps; search for weapons caches; body count; interrogation of prisoners; after-action reports. Paperwork, paperwork... yuck!

As for interrogation, some prisoners talk with a little coaching and of course, fear of torture and death, others are hard-core; they take a little more persuasion. You may or may not have heard of this method of interrogation, take a few blindfolded prisoners up in a helicopter to about one-hundred feet then descend slowly so they do not know they are only a few feet off the ground. Begin the questioning and threatening them that you will throw them out of the helicopter, one at a time until someone starts talking. Well, that's the way it is sometimes done and then there is another way, it goes the same as the aforementioned except there is no slow descent.

The ARVN interrogators took the prisoners up to about one-hundred feet and began questioning, when there was no cooperation, they pushed one of them out. The others began to talk. This tactic repeated a few more times until all the hard-cores had either talked or went sky diving. Over the remainder of the day the other prisoners were moved to a holding area where they would wait until evacuation could be arranged. Under normal circumstances captured prisoners and Chu Hoi are sent to a prison camp for repatriation and reprogramming.

On this day the circumstances would not be "normal." A while after moving the prisoners off to a holding area, out of our line of site, I was startled to hear burst after burst of machine gun fire. I was also surprised to see there was nobody scrambling, taking defensive positions. The machine gun bursts continued for a while and suddenly I knew from the direction of the noise, it was coming from the prisoner holding area. I quickly headed that direction and my way was almost instantly blocked by ARVN soldiers standing on the pathway that lead in that direction. I knew what had happened, there would be no evacuation, and the prisoners had been processed, so to speak. This did not set well with me; I went to my team leader and I was informed that we need not poke our noses into the matter. This would be handled by the ARVNs; we were not to concern ourselves with anything that we thought might have happened.

A few days later there was another VIP visit, another photo op for the brass. I had the opportunity to speak with Reb and I took him aside to tell him of what I had heard and what my suspicions were. At that point Reb cut the conversation abruptly. He glared straight at me with his steely blue eyes and said, "Sergeant, don't make waves!" I knew that it would behoove me to keep my mouth shut, I never mentioned it again.

All-in-all I feel very blessed to be sitting here writing these words. There were many close calls. At times I did some things that should have gotten me killed. My mother once told me, "Obviously God isn't done with you yet." Thanks Mom, I now know that she was right. There are 10s of thousands of fallen soldiers who never had to experience the rejection on their returning home. They didn't have the experience of night after night of reliving the "Nam Experience", waking up drenched in sweat or hollering themselves and their whole household awake. Needless to say I am grateful that for my journey home I was situated in the coach seat of the air craft and not inside an aluminum box stowed in the cargo hold of the aircraft.

"Let the morning bring me word of Your unfailing love, for I have put my trust in You. Show me the way I should go, for to You I lift up my soul." - Psalm 143:8

King David is the only man, to my knowledge, that God describes as a man after His own heart. If you know David's life story, he was a fearless young man who did some things that one might perceive as "stupid." David loved the Lord and trusted Him. There were stumbling blocks in David's life; many times they were a result of making poor choices. Even so David continually sought to know and do God's will in his life. Like many of us, David's will got in the way. Can you relate to David? I know that I certainly can relate.

God is not done with me and He is not done with you. We need to seek God's will for our lives and even though we may stumble and fall like David did, God will never forsake us. We need to firmly believe that.

Why did so many have to die in the war? Why did we live?

"For my thoughts are not your thoughts, neither are your ways my ways," declares the Lord, "As the heavens are higher than the earth, so are my ways higher than your ways and my thoughts than your thoughts." – Isaiah 155:8, 9

Why do I have no compassion for the lost and broken soldiers?

"Teach me to do Your will, for You are my God; may Your good Spirit lead me on level ground." - — Psalm 143:10

To God Be The Glory

Having engaged in combat in a variety of surroundings: rice paddies, swamps, jungles, Riverine operations near the Sugar Mill on the Song Vam Co Dong River (known to Naval

Riverine Ops as "The River of Death"), and last but not least the Nui Ba Den experience of Vietnam, I know that it was not providence that spared my life... I know that God had other plans for me.... To Him I give the glory and my undying gratitude!

My life was spared and my character was tested in ways that I never could have imagined. Incredibly I met men on the plane ride back to the U.S. who said that they missed Vietnam. I even expressed such feelings for a time after returning home. Only those of you who have experience combat and developed the intense camaraderie with your fellow soldiers could understand a statement like that. To those of you who have not experienced combat and been in direct fire, the statement sounds absolutely crazy.

I haven't tested my manhood by loading boots with the owner's foot still inside onto a Dust-Off chopper, but I have helped stack various detached limbs of enemy soldiers in an effort to get a body count for the infamous after action reports. I have, while under fire, dragged from the battlefield the body of fellow soldiers. Believe me, I don't miss that and I don't miss the incredible adrenaline rush that comes on you when you are engaged in an intense fire-fight or the unbelievable false sense of security you feel while standing on top of a tank, behind a 50 caliber, charging a wood line. You can actually hear and feel the bullets whizzing by you and be focused and unaffected by the danger of it all. Sounds crazy, doesn't it? What is even crazier to me is living life unaware of where you will spend eternity. Sound crazy to you? It is very sobering if you give it some thought.

The majority of people I went through training with at Fort Knox and Fort Sill during the 1969 to early 1970 time frame were almost entirely draftees. The fellow MACV Advisors I served with in Vietnam had volunteered for their tour of duty, as I had. I am still proud of the Advisory Team I served with and lived within our refuge, the house we built on the ARVN compound in Ap Tan My, not too awfully far from Trang Bang. These men weren't exactly my brothers, but in some ways we were even closer than brothers. I am equally proud of those ARVN soldiers I served with and fought alongside of, shoulder to shoulder in combat. They were tough and resilient against all odds. I am proud to have soldiered with them. Many of them lost their lives in combat, some men I considered friends, their faces are forever imprinted in my mind. They and their families wanted that war no more than we did. They were frightened young men, as most of us were, many of them were draftees. They could not dodge the draft as some young Americans were doing in those times. Our draft dodgers ran off to Canada, received a full pardon for desertion, and lived happily ever after. If a Vietnamese man were to refuse to serve, he would be imprisoned and serve hard labor for the duration of the war. Many draft dodgers and deserters were executed on the spot when caught. They had to fight against and kill their own countrymen, as none of us were forced to do.

Nobody who missed the Vietnam War should regret the fact. It was a waste of blood and time and treasure. It did no socioeconomic good of which I'm aware, and did a great deal of evil of which I'm far too aware. But having said that... I was called by my country and I served PROUDLY!

Chapter 6
The Black Hole

A **black hole** is a region of space in which the gravitational field is so powerful that nothing can escape. The name comes from the fact that even light is unable to escape, rendering the interior invisible. However, black holes can be detected if they interact with matter *outside* the event horizon, for example by drawing in gas from an orbiting star. The gas spirals inward, heating up to very high temperatures and emitting large amounts of radiation in the process.

You are probably asking yourself, "What the heck is the point here?" Well, my point is, there are some experiences in life that seem to draw us into an inescapable sphere. They are all consuming experiences that we will ostensibly never be able to leave in the past and move on with our lives.

THE AWAKENING

For some, these events of war are just memories of a time in life. For me they are mere shadows from a former life. Sometimes they even seem like memories that belong to a person other than me. It is hard for me to picture myself in those places, living out those unspeakable experiences. When I remember back, it's to some extent fuzzy and muddled. Some things I remember as clearly as if those experiences of war and carnage had taken place yesterday. The details, the images have remained with me for the more than thirty-five years of my life since I was in Vietnam and Cambodia. Fortunately there are some good memories that are intermingled with those other memories. It is those *"other"* memories that are more elusive. I'm not sure if the memories are somewhat vague because I can't remember or I tried to forget. In either case, as put these words to paper, I am reaching deeply into a place in my mind for those memories that have been locked away for years. They have been locked away tightly because subconsciously my mind is protecting me from the horrors that a combat soldier has lived through.

Where this process began was one day my daughter asked me if I would be willing to speak to her high school history class and recount to them what it was like to be a combat soldier fighting in the Vietnam War. At first I was a bit resistant to the proposition, but she went on to explain that her history teacher was interested in having veterans of WWII, the Korean War, and the Vietnam War come into the classroom, give a talk, and perhaps have a question and answer session at the end. The format would be whatever the Vet felt be comfortable with.

I hesitantly agreed to participate and began almost immediately to put words on paper. I found myself recalling things I had not spoken of in years and even some things I had never spoken of. As I relived some of those experiences they were so vivid that I could feel my chest tighten and they brought tears to my eyes. I began to wake at night, reliving the war. They were back again, those same nightmares that plagued me for such a long time after returning to the "real world" from the jungles and rice paddies of Vietnam.

Through this process I believe I was able to unload some baggage that I had been unaware of, baggage I had been carrying with me for years. One very impacting experience is something that as I look back, brought a deep shame to me. The year was 1993; I was visiting the Washington D.C. area on a work related trip. It was the Easter vacation week so I took the opportunity to bring my family along with me. We arrived on the weekend and had some time to sight-see so we decided to go down to the Capitol Mall area and visit the monuments and museums. I had never seen the Vietnam War Memorial so we decided that we would go to The Wall. I wanted to visit the Wall for two reasons, first to see the polished black granite wall that honored the thousands who had made the ultimate sacrifice for their country and the people of Vietnam, second to look for the name of my dear friend, Gary Brown who had been killed in action just a few short months after arriving in Vietnam. I often feel that Gary died in my place. If you don't recall the incident, go back to chapter 3 where it is explained.

Now, getting back to my train of thought; as I approached the monument I felt an overwhelming sense of awe. I am not sure if I had a mental picture of what I expected to see, but let me tell you, if you have never been to the Vietnam Memorial in DC, my jaw dropped. The enormity of that shiny black wall was all engulfing; I could barely take my eyes off of it. I could see people milling about and many standing before the polished black wall; some were kneeling as if to pray. There was a quiet reverence about the Wall and the area surrounding the monument. I felt a deep sense that this was hallowed ground. Walls are built as barriers meant to separate, but this wall was built to bring people together. It was erected to commemorate the lives lost in a land far, far away. This wall helped in some ways to heal the wounds of the generations that were divided because of the war.

At the time of my visit the wall contained the names of 57,939 fallen soldiers who had gone to war. They were sons and daughters of a generation who were proud of their patriotism; they were dedicated to their country and what it stood for. These soldiers answered the call, not questioning the authority of those who called them to war and trained them to obey their superiors with unquestioning loyalty.

As I approached the wall, off to the side I caught sight of a man dressed in camouflage jungle fatigues, the same style that I wore "in country", Vietnam. He appeared to be about the same age as me at the time. I notice that he was holding a sign that read, "Homeless, Vietnam Vet, Please Help." Now, on any other day, in any other place, I would have ignored the man and just silently walked past him as if he didn't exist. On this day, however, I felt obligated to acknowledge him, so I walked up and stood squarely in front of him and I said, "I'm a Vietnam Vet too, why don't you just get over it!" He just looked at me in shock and said nothing. I turned and walked away, feeling all smug and even a bit self-satisfied.

This memory is one of those that bring tears to my eyes even today. The tears come from the coldness I felt as I remembered and relived that moment. I felt chilled to the bones for having seen the ugliness inside of me. Instead of feeling compassion for a brother who had gone through the hell that I had, I handed him a virtual slap in the face.

As I summoned up the visions and feelings of that day years before, it was right then and there that God squeezed my heart; I felt it break in my chest. I felt a deep shame for the way I had treated that Vet and shame for the distain I had felt for those many years for any of those who, for whatever reason, were unable to cope with what they had lived through. For those who had maybe never even seen combat but still felt a deep remorse and shame for being a part of the enormous war machine that had wreaked havoc on the people of Vietnam. Some of those soldiers came home feeling a deep anger, and some came home feeling guilty that so many had died and they had survived.

There are myriads of events too numerous to cite that impacted these broken soldiers. These events continue to leave them embittered and frustrated with themselves and their trials continue to shape their lives today. My hope is that some of them might be reading these word that are meant to point them to a place of hope and the beginning of a healing that can take place in their hearts.

I wish that someday I might go back to the Wall and see that vet and hand him a copy of this book. I want so much to apologize to him for my cold and shameful behavior. I want to sit and talk with him and try to understand what it is or was that he could not let go of. What was it that left him a *broken soldier*? The reality of it is that I will probably never see him again, so perhaps the act of writing this book and the experience at the Wall which has given me a contrite heart will serve as an act of forgiveness for my harsh words.

BROKENNESS TO WHOLENESS

When we are broken, wholeness can seem unattainable. No matter what the degree of hopelessness you might feel from the proverbial black hole you have been pulled into, there is hope and there is a way out. We need to grasp onto that hope and begin the search for wholeness. Wholeness is not found by focusing on one's own problems, rather wholeness can be achieved through reaching out and giving of one's self. There is a need for a starting point; you must not conclude that you have nothing to give. You can give by serving others, even if you have never served. You can show compassion to others, I was able to come to grips with my apathy toward the veterans and the many other broken people who, in my opinion, could not control their emotions. My attitude was, "just get a grip and get on with life." It is so easy to allow ourselves to fall into that way of thinking… that trap.

Our desperate search for hope often takes us on a journey to find that which we have never known. Our determination to find what was lost only causes us to lose our way. The search for wholeness is counterintuitive and requires us to let go of what we so long to take hold of and to begin a pilgrimage that leads us to an entirely different path. Wholeness is not found through receiving, but through giving. This is why wholeness and generosity are inseparably linked. It is easy to conclude, I cannot give what I do not have. While it is true you cannot give what you do not have, you can give what you have not experienced. From a purely human perspective, you can serve even if you've never been served; you can forgive even if you've never been forgiven; you can express compassion even if you're never received compassion. Yet when most of us conclude we have nothing to give, it is based on an evaluation of what we've experienced.

Are you in a virtual Black Hole? In 2 Corinthians 12:9 the Apostle Paul asked God to remove a trial from his life and the answer that Paul received was "My grace is sufficient for you, for my power is made perfect in weakness." In other words, when we are under pressure that seems to be unbearable, when we feel far from God and no sense of His presence in our lives... that is when He may be drawing us near to Him.

Have you ever questioned the reality of God? Have you ever questioned whether He really loves you? When you feel the farthest from Him God will show His presence through someone or through a situation that will occur in our lives. These events are faith experiences and God does them in every person's life to call us into a relationship with Him or to call us to a higher level of relationship with Him. God is persistent and He seeks U.S. out, if only we have ears to hear Him and eyes to see Him.

"My grace is sufficient." Do those word ring true to you in your life? This could be a starting point for you. This could be the place, right here and now, where you begin the process of stepping out of the Black Hole (**brokenness**) and into the Light (**wholeness**) that comes from our Maker.

Chapter 7
The Longest Night

TET – 1971

Nui Ba Den rises 3000 feet, (1000 meters) above the rice paddies and jungles of Tay Ninh Province north and west of Ho Chi Minh city, (formerly Saigon, the capitol city of South Vietnam), 18 miles from the border of Cambodia. A granite uprising, jutting from the flatlands that surround it and covered with jungle, this ancient volcano has, for centuries, been a very powerful symbol of folk lore and in modern-day wars a military strategic point.

There are several stories as to how the ancient volcano received its name. A common version that dates prior to the 1700s; a local chieftain had a daughter, Nang Denh. A Chinese Buddhist monk who was passing through the area asked the local chieftain if he could stay and live in the area and practice the teachings of Buddha. The Chieftain agreed and the monk built a temple called Chua Ong Tau (Chinese Monks Temple), the ruins of which can still be seen at the foot of the eastern slopes of the mountain. In time, Nang Denh became a devoted follower of Buddhism. When her father offered her in marriage to a neighboring Chieftains son, Nang Denh resisted and went into hiding on the mountain. She was never seen again and it was thought she killed herself rather than leave her life of Buddhism.

Years later a different priest was said to have seen Nang Denh walking along the mountain slopes. In recognition of Nang Denh, the priest built an alter; the Shrine of the Black Virgin which still stands on the mountain side.

I have read that Nui Ba Den translates to Black Virgin Mountain and Black Widow Mountain but from all that I have read, the most accurate translation is Black Lady Mountain. At the base of Nui Ba Den and to the North West is a smaller mountain, Nui Caw or the "Saddle", as those stationed in the mountain top base camp, referred to it.

Many times while the rice paddies and jungles surrounding Nui Ba Den were being drenched in torrential rain, the summit would be in perfectly clear weather. Conversely there were times the surrounding area would be having a full day of sun, and there would be a dense cloud covering the summit, so thick that at times the helicopter pilots were not able to land. All supplies had to be delivered by helicopter and at times supplies would not arrive for days until the weather at the summit cleared.

Some soldiers thought the summit base camp was a safe place while others thought they were very vulnerable, only able to safely remain there until the VC or NVA thought otherwise. In any case the view from the summit base camp was fantastic. Sunrise and sunset was nothing less than a breath taking experience.

The enemy advantage was their ability to closely approach and break into the perimeter, sometimes undetected and their thorough knowledge of the locations of key installations such as VHF antenna towers, living quarters, and the generators.

Was it true, what I had been told? The base camp atop Nui Ba Den had been overrun during Tet, the Chinese New Year, and every year since 1968. At the time I did not concern myself with the claim, which to me was just a pathetic assertion meant solely for the purpose of scaring the newbie, namely me.

Rewind with me for a moment while my thoughts digress... I need to set the stage for the next sub-chapter.

I had thought I would be beating the bush with the ARVNs for a year, that is if a well aimed enemy bullet or the shrapnel from a B-40 rocket or mortar shell didn't get me first. As a the advisory team's Heavy Weapons Advisor my job, theoretically, was to help the ARVN mortar men become more proficient at their craft of killing NVA and Viet Cong with expertly delivered mortar shells. The only problem with the plan was that it was only a "theoretical" plan. I had never received the advanced training that Infantrymen go through and I had never handled a mortar or even been exposed to the skills it takes to set-up and fire a mortar tube. My advanced training was in Field Artillery and I had learned to set-up and fire every conceivable piece of artillery that was current during the Vietnam era. I was trained as an Artillery Crew Chief; 13B40 was my MOS when I deployed to Southeast Asia from Fort Lewis, Washington on February 12, 1970. My original orders were for me to report to Camp Eagle located near Phu Bi, I Corp. The fire support base was situated on the picturesque DMZ between North and South Vietnam.

While in training at Fort Sill, Oklahoma I had learned how to set-up, fire, breakdown, clean, and even remove and replace the drive train of self-propelled howitzers. There was the 105 mm. and the 155 mm. towed howitzers and the self-propelled (tank-like tracked vehicles) howitzers; the 105 mm., 155 mm., and the 175 mm. additionally there was my absolute favorite field artillery weapon, the self-propelled 8-inch gun.... what a sweet piece of technology with matchless accuracy.

With well trained crews a battery of 8-inch guns, M110A2 can deliver ordinance, a 200 pound projectile, at a rate of 8 rounds per minute at distances up to 18 miles. The projectile leaves the barrel at a muzzle velocity of 2300 feet/second, breaking the sound barrier very shortly after leaving the end of the barrel. There actually is a double BANG when a round is fired, one bang as the gunpowder ignites and the second bang sounds as the shell breaks to speed of sound (1125 feet/second), followed by a large smoke ring..... quite a sight to see.

THANKS BUT NO THANKS

One of my first official acts as the Heavy Weapons Advisor was to visit the ARVN artillery battery that was located at the furthermost outskirts of our battalion compound. My thought was that artillery cannons were "heavy weapons" and that was my expertise. I later learned what my job really was and it was not to meddle with the ARVN artillery battery.

I wanted to let the artillery Battery Commander, (BC) know that I had arrived and I wanted him to know that I was available to him and the artillerymen for training and tips on the care and feeding of his battery of 105 mm., towed howitzers. The BC was cordial and at the same time curious as to why I showed such an interest in him and his crew. He gave me the 50 cent tour of the battery and then sent me on my way; I got the impression that his sentiments were "thanks but no thanks" on my offer to share my wealth of knowledge with him and his crew. I was later informed that in the Infantry mortar launchers and 106 mm. recoilless rifles are considered heavy weapons...... Okaaaay!

Sometime after my first meeting with the BC of the artillery battery I was out in the field beating the bushes in the infamous Iron Triangle with one of our ARVN companies. The location of the Iron Triangle was between the Saigon River on the west and the Tinh River on the east and bordering Route 13 about 25 miles (40 km) north of Saigon. The southern apex of the "triangle" was seven miles (11 km) from Phu Cong, the capital of Binh Duong Province. Its proximity to Saigon was both a reason for American and South Vietnamese efforts to eradicate the enemy within the area and destroy its extensive tunnel and bunker systems, as well as why it remained a crucial area for Communist forces to maintain control over.

The Iron Triangle earned its notoriety from a 1967 battle that raged for 19-days. Operation Cedar Falls was an especially intensive attack involving nearly 16,000 American troops and an ARVN combat force of 14,000. The Operation took nineteen days, during which 72 Americans, 11 ARVNs, and 720 Viet Cong were killed. Despite their massive attack with B-52 bombers, tanks with bulldozer blades and efforts to destroy the tunnel systems by explosives, flooding and "tunnel rats"(specially trained soldiers who would infiltrate the tunnels armed only with a flashlight and a handgun), the Americans failed to totally destroy the Viet Cong support system that had been built for over two decades.

Anyway, back the story, we had made contact with what appeared to be a sizable enemy unit. I recommended to the ARVN company commander that we consider calling for fire support to help soften the enemy unit. The Captain agreed and I quickly got on the PRC25 field radio to call for artillery support. Since we were in a fairly close proximity to our base camp the fire support came from our very own artillery battery. When I made contact with the BC I gave him our location and the grid coordinates of the enemy and as is SOP, I requested that a marking round be fired. Marking rounds are normally an air-burst of a smoke round to verify that the grid coordinates given are accurate and that the howitzers firing are aimed properly. Well, the marking round delivered was not what we expected and it didn't drop where we intended. The first round fired was a high-explosive round and it was not an air-burst. It was a point detonating round, which means that it explodes on contact with the ground or other hard surfaces.

The round dropped well short of the enemy position and it exploded dangerously close to our position. I called back and adjusted the coordinates to a point that I knew to be beyond the enemy position and then after verifying that the next round fired was reasonably close to where I wanted it to be I asked them to walk the next round and next rounds back toward the enemy position. Soon we were delivering salvos of artillery shells right on top of Charlie.

When I got back to our base camp the next day I went straight to the ARVN battalion commander, Thieu Ta (Major) Ba, to report that the artillery support very nearly took out our own troops. I wanted complete cooperation from Phao Doi Truong (battery commander) Thanhg. I requested that I be permitted to inspect the set-up of the howitzers in his artillery battery and I also wanted teach the cannon crew the proper way of setting up their howitzers for both daylight and night time shooting.

Please forgive me for rambling. That was a long story to get to my point, which is, soon after these events I just described I realized exactly what the REAL role of the Heavy Weapons Advisor was on this particular advisory team. I also realized why I had been chosen to serve with a MACV combat team rather than going to where my original order indicated, Camp Eagle. Rather than serve as an artilleryman in Phu Bi, I was serving with the ARVN Infantry as a Forward Observer, code name "Heavy Weapons Advisor."

Please fast forward with me now to the real point of this chapter, this time I really mean it!

Another Day in Paradise

It was just another day like any other on the mountain. My daily chores were to run system tests on the ARP signal converter and to complete the log books on any activity that had occurred the night before from anti-personnel sensors that might have been activated by the movement of enemy troops. These sensors were deployed as a part of the White Igloo program, which was my sole reason for being located on top of Nui Ba Den. The White Igloo program had been implemented sometime during 1968 under the direction of General William Westmoreland, Commander of troops stationed in Vietnam. A variety of electronic sensors had been deployed throughout South Vietnam on perimeters of military installations, along convoy routes and across principal enemy avenues of approach and infiltration zones and strategic points along the Song Vam Co Dong River. These sensors were devices that could be triggered by sound, motion, and seismic activity monitored. By the intensity of the transmission from a triggered sensor, information regarding number of people moving in the area and whether or not they were carrying weapons. All in all the technology was quite amazing. The sensors were very successful at monitoring enemy movements and identifying targets for artillery and air strikes. Tactical units and Special Forces teams of both the U.S. and ARVN forces monitored the sensors. To aid in the communication of readings from remote areas, a radio relay aircraft orbited the tri- border area west of Pleiku and a ground relay operated from the top of Nui Ba Den.

Since the U.S. 25th Infantry Division had redeployed as a part of the "Vietnam-ization" of the war, they had pulled out of Cu Chi base camp and the ARVN 25th Infantry Division had assumed all responsibilities that the U.S. had supported. My civilian schooling in electronics technology had won me the recognition of my senior officers and the prize was an all-expenses paid trip to paradise. This beautiful base camp located atop a magnificent mountain (probably the only mountain) in III Corp, was surrounded in a picturesque setting of lush green, dense jungle a comfortable distance from scenic Tay Ninh City.

At the very top of Nui Ba Den there was a pagoda, a shrine of sorts built to honor the Cambodian princess that legend said had taken her life on the mountain. Inside the pagoda there was a painted and sealed concrete vault of sorts, it reminded me of an Egyptian sarcophagus. It was ornately painted with something that, I guess, was supposed to be the likeness of a Cambodian princess. We knew never to disturb the pagoda or its contents.

From atop the Black Virgin Pagoda one would have a breath taking view of the surrounding countryside. We had ring-side seats, an eagle's eye view of the goings on down below. Sometimes we would go up and sit on the deck over top of the pagoda and "watch the war" as we referred to it.

Now and then, during the day light hours, you might have a false sense that you were removed from the dangers of war. As dusk approached you would tend to take on a different attitude, for we knew that Charlie owned the mountain and we remained at the top at his pleasure, so to speak. On one side of the deck was a 50 caliber machine gun, rigged for single shot. The machine gun was equipped with a large and powerful starlight scope. The scope gave you the ability to monitor any movement on Nui Caw, the saddle off the side of the mountain. Sometimes you would see enemy soldiers moving around at night on the saddle. It was a rare occurrence because I am sure that after a number of them getting picked off by the 50 caliber, they knew not to move through the area within the view of the deadly machine gun. There was a sign-up sheet for the machine gun with 30 minute time slots. I sat up there a few times but never saw movement. The deck and the 50 caliber was another reason that Charlie wanted to take the pagoda out, permanently.

Nui Ba Den base camp; Helicopter Pad in the foreground; Black Virgin Pagoda in the background. My bunker/hooch was located a bit down the mountain, directly in behind and to the left of the Pagoda (top-center), as pictured.

I was the only MACV soldier on the mountain; the other 20 or so U.S. soldiers were from various military units. Their main duties revolved around radio communications. The occupation of Nui Ba Den was a strategic advantage to U.S. forces in III Corp, Vietnam. The mountain base camp served as a radio relay center for many combat and support units scattered throughout South Vietnam. Also located on the base camp there were two companies, approximately four hundred ARVN soldiers.

The job of the ARVN soldiers was to ensure the security of the base camp by engaging the enemy on any attempts to compromise our perimeter or invade/overrun our base camp perimeter. The base camp was set up with an outer perimeter and an inner perimeter. The ARVNs occupied the area between the outer perimeter and the wire of the inner perimeter. Co-located with the ARVN soldiers were the families of many of the soldiers. The families lived on the base camp as was the custom on any ARVN base camp I'd ever set foot on. It was convenient for the ARVNs as well as the Americans, since some of the ARVN wives provided laundry service for the U.S. contingent located within the inner perimeter of the base camp.

Wash day on Nui Ba Den.
Wives of ARVN soldiers hang wash.

Since the beginning of Tet (The Chinese New Year) we were on heightened security. There was an uneasy awareness of what surprises Tet could bring. Everyone on the mountain knew the history of what Tet meant for the mountain top occupants of years past. Some spoke of times gone by regarding the history of Tet and the mountain and yet others avoided discussing or even hearing the stories, almost as if they were in denial that anything like that ever happened. We had noticed an increase in activity from our unwelcomed neighbors who lived outside the perimeter wire. The NVA and Vietcong basically owned the entire mountain, except for the top. They were beginning to harass us more frequently by night. There would be the almost laughable bull horn broadcasts aimed at demoralizing their unwanted mountain top occupants... us! Little did they know that the broadcasts were actually sort of comical to us. Then there were the not so comical barrages of mortar shells that were launched more frequently these days. The mortar shelling most often occurred during the hours of darkness.

1 Pagoda and Communications Bunker
2 My Bunker (Conex)
3 ARP Sig. Converter Bunker
4 Communications Building
5 Latrine
6 Mess Hall
7 U.S. Billets
8 U.S. Billets
9 U.S. Billets
10 U.S. Billets
11 Officer Housing

12 Officer & Enlisted Men's Club
13 Medical Bunker
14 Shower House
15 Day Room
16 Special Forces Billets
17 Orderly Room
18 Generator Shed
19 Emergency Helicopter Pad
20 Water Resivoir
21 Primary Helicopter Pad
22 Mortar Pit

Nui Ba Den Base camp Layout

It had been several days since the start of Tet, which begins with the New Moon on the first day of the New Year and ends on the full moon 15 days later. This particular night was unnerving because sappers had snuck through the perimeter wire and blown up our generator with satchel charges. The bad guys were quickly flushed out and exterminated by the ARVN perimeter guards. Questions came up later regarding as to just how the bad guys were able to navigate the outside mine field and compromise our perimeter of barbed wire and razor wire. There were some grumblings among the U.S.

troops and especially with the two Green Berets who were among the 20 or so U.S. contingent on the mountain. The Berets wanted to challenge and investigate the perimeter security plans. After much discussion it was decided that there could be a serious backlash from the ARVN command. It was a very tense time and emotions could have led to ugliness and bloodshed between comrades. It was decided by the U.S. base camp commander to not push issues any further.

We were able to get through the rest of the night and the next day with several back-up generators scattered throughout the base camp. Two days after the sappers had taken out our main generator a huge Chinook Helicopter delivered a new generator, which was quickly put into operation.

Lord – "Please Don't Let The Daylight End"

Everyone was edgy; our destiny seemed to be completely out of our control. There was quiet talk among the U.S. troops concerning our vulnerability. In essence we were inside of a compound surrounded by mine fields and several perimeter rings of razor wire and tangle foot, but even though by all military standards our perimeter was secure, we still felt that we were actually behind enemy lines. If Charlie came through the wire, if we were overrun and out gunned, where would we go? There was nowhere to retreat to and there was nowhere to hide.

Some of you, as you read these words, if you've been in a similar predicament, you can begin to feel that familiar tightening of the chest and sickening in your stomach. That is exactly what each of us was feeling. I recalled a similar feeling of when as a child. I had my first experience at being sent to the Principal's office. I was ushered by the school secretary into the Principal's office, who at the time was not in his office. I was instructed to sit in a chair and wait for the Principal to return. The wait was agonizing, I felt sick inside, as though I might just throw up all over the carpet.

As the day wore on, I believe that most of us felt a similar sickening agony inside. Everyone was uptight. There was little to no conversation, only what was necessary to conduct operations. The usual light-hearted joking was non-existent. Each person was focused on his own thoughts. Although no one actually said it, I believe that each of us felt as if this might well be our last day to draw breath in this life.

Have you ever felt a complete sense of hopelessness? While on the battle field I had never really felt this way, which is because my emotions were both fueled and numbed by adrenalin. In this situation you have time to contemplate your mortality and your imagination runs wild. It is an all-consuming experience that, if you allow it to overtake your consciousness it can suck the very life out of you. Can you relate?

As sunset drew near, I retreated to my bunker cleaning, checking and rechecking my M-16 rifle. I verified that the

Claymore mines that I had situated in the corridor that led from the outside to door of my sandbagged aluminum conex were correctly wired to a hand crank generator. I also verified that each mine was aimed so as to inflict maximum damage to anyone who entered that corridor with intent to do harm to me. That's right; I lived in a metal box that was covered with about 40 layers of sandbags on all sides and on top. There two Claymore mines located along the 15 foot corridor between the outer door and inner door of my mountain top sanctuary. The mines could be detonated from inside the conex; they were intended as my last line of defense in case the enemy made it through wire and overran our compound. On top of my bunker was a machine gun nest of sorts, fashioned from wooden ammo crates and sandbags. I made sure I had an ample supply of hand grenades and ammo, which I hoped I would not need that night or any night, for that matter.

As darkness fell, I withdrew to my bunker. I locked and secured the outer door to my bunker and then entered my conex, locking and securing the heavy metal inner door. Now the long wait began. There I sat, inside a big aluminum box. Thoughts of another aluminum box flashed through my mind, I had visions of the shiny military caskets lined up on a tarmac waiting to be loaded on an aircraft that would take the fallen soldiers inside of those boxes on their final journey home. Would I end up in one of those boxes? Would anyone even be able to find my body? Would I be taken prisoner or executed? Would I go out in a blaze of glory and machine gun fire?

As I sat there trying to concentrate and run through plans in my head I found it hard to focus on what action I would take with regard to various scenarios that played out in my mind. I recalled a briefing I attended my first day on the mountain. During the briefing the commanding officer of the U.S. contingent of the base camp said something that played back over and over in my head as I sat there in my bunker hopelessly trying to concentrate. The C/O had instructed us that if our outer perimeter was breached, no one, absolutely no one was allowed to come through the perimeter wire of the inner-most compound where the U.S. personnel resided. We were ordered to shoot to kill anyone who tried to enter the inner compound of our mountain top base camp. Since our outer perimeter guards were Vietnamese and our enemy was also Vietnamese, we had no way to verify whether anyone attempting to enter the inner compound was friend or foe.

Our ARVN perimeter guards and their commanding officers were briefed on the same subject and they fully understood that they were NOT to enter the inner compound at any time unless it was on prearranged official business with the U.S. commander.

I opened my Bible, the one given to me by the Gideons on the day I was officially inducted into the Army. I don't recall any particular passages I tried to read but I knew that somehow verses of God's Word would comfort me. I remember looking in the front of the book for verses related to anxiety and loneliness. There were other dark moments of the war for me, but this time it seemed to be the darkest moment. This time it was different. During other battles there was sometimes that tinge of fear that lasted only for a moment before engagement. Then you operated on pure adrenalin and the training that the Drill Instructors had barked into you head. The training, at the time, seemed to be only worthless harassment, but when the stuff hit the fan you remembered what you needed to do... you operated on well programmed instinct.

The same went for my church schooling on Sunday mornings. At the time it occasionally seemed unimportant, dull and boring, but now it was very real, God's Word was very real to me. I felt as if there was no hope, but hope was what I was looking for in the Holy Scriptures. I can't recall now what my exact feelings were but I do recall that the comfort I looked for in God's Word must have been found because after a time, I don't know how long, I drifted off to sleep, safe in the arms of God.

Zero-Dark 30

Suddenly I awoke with a start... as I drifted into consciousness I realized that the warning alarm was sounding at full volume, we were under attack! I awoke to complete darkness; the small red indicator lights that were connected to the ARP signal converter relays that I maintained and monitored were not lit. That meant the main generator must have been knocked out. As I fumbled in the darkness to locate my flashlight I could hear random explosions and the rat-ta-tat-tat of machine gun fire. Was this a dream? My instincts quickly told me "NO, this is for real!" My senses almost instantly kicked in to auto-pilot mode, we were under attack! I jumped up and grabbed my M-16. I listened closely to be sure that there was no action taking place immediately outside my bunker. I unlocked my doors and as quietly as I could, made my way up to my machine gun nest atop my bunker. One of the first things I noticed as I came out of my bunker was that the Pagoda was ablaze on one side, I later learned that it had been hit by a B-40 rocket. I could see that some of the perimeter lights had been knocked out and there was some pretty intense action going on outside and inside the outer perimeter. My mind echoed, "Oh my God, Charlie has broken through and they are inside the wire." I waited and I prayed. I didn't have to wait for very long before I could see that the fire-fights were getting closer, green tracers and red tracers seemed to be flying in every direction. I intently kept an eye the inner perimeter wire, waiting and watching for anyone who might attempt to come through. Any lights that were left were out in the distance on the outer perimeter, they did little good to help my close field of view. There were occasional volleys of flares sent up by the U.S. to help illuminate the battlefield. Every once in a while I'd catch a glimpse of a pith helmet so I knew that it was NVA regulars that had come through the wire. It was hard to see from my vantage point if anyone was attempting to come into the inner compound. Suddenly I heard movement; there were the sounds of scuffling and the sounds of clanging metal. I could see no movement but I could hear and find a direction for the sound, it was nearby and almost directly in front of me.

For all of my years growing up and learning to hunt I had always learned, "verify your target!" On the military rifle ranges, same thing, "verify you target!" What I was about to do went against everything I has learned, but the C/O's words during the newbie first day briefing rang out, "No one, absolutely no one is allowed to come through the perimeter of the inner compound!" I didn't want to fire my M-16 in fear that I might give away my position. I pulled the pin and lobbed a hand grenade in the direction of sounds out in front of me. Instantly with the explosion I heard a commotion followed by hollering, screaming and the sounds of scrambling. I pointed my rifle into the darkness, in the direction of the sound, said a quick prayer and squeeze the trigger, ripping off a few short bursts, more scuffling and metallic clicking sounds, so I just held the trigger until the magazine emptied and I reloaded. I pulled pins and lobbed another grenade or two; I continued firing short bursts toward sounds coming from different directions in front of me, spraying bullets back and forth. I could hear intermittently, bullets whizzing by and bullets striking sandbags and the big granite rock behind me, the huge granite rock that was the base of the Black Virgin Pagoda. I kept thinking in my mind, "If only I could call on Helicopter Gunships or Artillery for fire support to get me out of this mess." The only reality of that moment that I could see in my mind was that all I had was instinct and military survival training... that was it... the only thing I could call on!

I realize today that I had the strength of my faith to call on, but what I was facing at that moment had me so fearful that my mind could not focus on the strength that was within me, the Holy Spirit was with me and for whatever reason, panic did not overtake me. I was able to call on those learned military defensive instincts to keep me on track, engaging the enemy in close range combat.

The fire-fight with the faceless enemy went on in the darkness for I don't know how long. All around me I could hear the staccato of automatic weapons fire, there was the distinct popping sound of the AK-47. Explosions, unintelligible yelling, and chaos were all around me. All of a sudden I heard another alarm, DEFCON (defensive condition). That alarm signal meant we were to take cover immediately and hunker down... close range defensive artillery or air strikes were about to commence. I had never experienced DEFCON on the mountain, I was unsure of exactly what was about to take place but I knew I must take cover and quickly. I fired a few more short bursts, spraying the entire area in front of me, by this time I had emptied several magazines of ammo.

I lobbed another grenade, which gave me precious little time to quickly withdraw from the machine gun nest. I scurried, half falling and sliding my way down to the entrance to my bunker. I hurriedly secured the outer door and scurried down the corridor, slamming and locking the conex door behind me.

I sat in darkness on my bunk with my M-16 in hand. I had no way of knowing what would happen next. I had to keep telling myself, this was not a training exercise, this was for REAL! I did not want to turn on my flashlight for I wanted my night vision to be as sharp as possible. I felt in the darkness for the Claymore mine hand generators that hung on the wall where I had them arranged in order of closest to the outer door to nearest to my conex. This was it, I felt like I was in a sardine can and Charlie had the P-38 can opener. I waited and again I began to pray. The words of Hebrews 13:5 kept running through my head; *"I will never leave you or forsake you."* The words and the thought brought calmness to me, but the calming was short lived. I could hear the sounds of the enemy outside of my bunker. The sounds were those of preying and banging at the outer door of the corridor, they were coming to get me! Oh, my God, please save me!

As I sat in the darkness carefully clutching a hand generator and waiting for the noises to cease I formed mental pictures in my head. I tried hard to visualize Charlie and when would be the optimum moment to detonate the first Claymore. The noises ceased, I waited just a moment... I squeezed the hand generator.

M18A1 Claymore Anti-Personnel Mine

Description *– The M18A1 anti-personnel mine is a fragmentation munition that contains 700 steel balls and 682 grams of C4 plastic explosive. It can be detonated by command via electric or nonelectric blasting caps. The Claymore is a one-shot weapon. It is primarily designed for use against massed infantry attacks. The mine is largely employed as a defensive weapon and its use is limited only by the imagination of the user. When detonated, the M18A1 mine will deliver its* *spherical steel fragments over a 60° fan-shaped pattern that is 2 meters high and 50 meters wide at a range of 50 meters. The weapon is extremely lethal within the 50 meter range.*

As I squeeze the hand-generator I felt a surge of hope from within. Then the deafening explosion followed by silence. In my mind's eye I could see the steel balls tearing through the enemy, ripping flesh, splintering bones, inflicting maximum lethal casualties. In reality I had no way of knowing if the claymore had any effect on Charlie.

After the deafening explosion I heard only silence for a few moments, and then I heard voices and what sounded like movement outside of or inside of the corridor. I grabbed the next hand generator and squeezed; another deafening blast and then silence... silence for what seemed to last minutes, then I heard them again, there was movement or something off to the side of my bunker... I had forgotten, there was another way into the conex. The armored window hatch was shut and locked. I heard the scraping and prying noises that sounded like someone prying the heavy metal screening that covered the small tunnel/air passage that ran between the window hatch and the outside of my bunker.

Those slimy little bastards were not going to give up. They were going to try to get to me through the window tunnel. I grabbed my M-16 and as quietly as I could, I opened the armored window hatch. Slowly, so as to not make noise and give any warning, I raised my M-16 to the window opening. I squeezed off several short bursts with my rifle to scramble the enemy. Instantly my ears were ringing. I slammed the window hatch closed and waited and tried listen. The ringing in my ears made it hard to detect whether or not sounds were real or imagined. It wasn't long before they were back at it again, real sounds and they were determined to gain access to my bunker and make me pay for any casualties I had caused to their comrades. I probably could have dwelt on what my fate would be, but there was no time for that.... focus, stay focused.... self-preservation was my main objective. I could not let panic set in. Fear and panic can paralyze you; I could not let that happen.

Unexpectedly and without warning I heard powerful explosions that seemed to be all around the base camp. These explosions were formidable, much stronger than the ones I had been hearing. Was it Artillery? Was it B-52 Bombers? Whatever it was it made the mountain shake, I could feel the rumble all around me in my bunker. Another sound I heard was the yelling and scrambling of the enemy on the outside of my bunker. Had they abandoned their quest to make me pay? It sounded as if they had suspended their efforts to get to me through the window hatch tunnel. Praise the Lord, my prayers were answered? Not a time to rush to judgment, just sit tight for a bit.

The explosions went on for a time; I sat in darkness for what seemed an eternity. I was numb to any kind of feeling. No feelings of elation, no sense of security crept into my mind. Would the next round fall on my bunker? Was Charlie still out there? I had no way of knowing what to do next. The strong

explosions had stopped. I expected to hear an all clear signal but there was none that I could hear. I sat for what seemed an hour. I resolved to believe it was over and the bad guys were all dead and gone.

Cautiously I opened the door to my conex. The door creaked as I opened it and I instantly stiffened, waiting to hear a shot or an explosion but none came. I heard sounds outside, people talking and yelling in English. I exited my bunker and saw the flicker of fire reflecting off the large granite boulder immediately outside my door. I heard the sounds of a large helicopter and looking over my bunker I could see a giant CH-47 (Chinook Helicopter). It was carrying a dumpster sized bucket of water to extinguish the flames of the pagoda and other buildings that had been set on fire.

I made my way down to the ARP Signal Converter bunker and saw that there had been some minor damage; one of the ARPs would have to be replaced. I watch, still numb from what had just happened. The Chinooks made sortie after sortie with the large buckets of water, extinguishing the fires. This all took place, as I recall, as daylight began to break over the horizon. The base camp was a mess. The corridor to my conex was a mess and in serious need of repair. By the amount of blood and other stuff I saw, the claymores had put a big hurt on Charlie. I thought to myself that perhaps they might come back again sometime and if they did, they'd have a bone to pick with me.

Thank God, that day never came while I was still on the mountain. There were the occasional lobbing of mortars and harassment schemes that went on but nothing as serious as what we had all experienced.

After action reports determined that a couple of our perimeter guards had likely been NVA sympathizers or they had been compromised by threats to their families or something like that. I am not sure what the truth was but I know that the after action reports never considered that Charlie had made it through because they knew, in detail, our perimeter layout and perhaps they had taken the perimeter guard captive or cut their throats. Miraculously there were no U.S. casualties. There were ARVN KIAs and wounded, and two perimeter guards unaccounted for.

Whatever happened, it is history. The rest of my days on the mountain were basically uneventful. I received and installed a replacement ARP converter and carried on sensor monitoring and daily activity reporting... and counting my days before I would leave this God forsake place for ever. The day seemed to drag on as I checked off each of my remaining days in country and on this mountain..... SHORT! That is typically what a soldier yells from time to time as his DROS day approaches. I made sure they all knew that my exit day was soon coming.

Major snag... I was still on the mountain and yesterday was the day I was supposed to leave. No helicopters could land on the mountain and no aircraft could do any fly-bys close to the mountain. Charlie was doing target practice with heavy machine guns. B-52s blanket bombed the Saddle and sides of the mountain a couple of times and finally after five days the bad guys were either taken out by bombing and artillery or they just decided to cease and desist for the time being in shooting at approaching aircraft.

Finally, after six extra days on the mountain I would be able to catch a ride on the mail chopper as it returned to Cu Chi base camp. I had been sweating it out for those six days, thinking that all hell would break loose again and I would end up on a list of KIAs in the after action report.

We made it safely to the helipad at Cu Chi base camp; a jeep picked me up and transported me and my gear to a transient hooch, since I had no permanent quarters on the ground base camp. I had paperwork to complete and steps to go through to process out of the country to the USA but, I was sick… very sick. It began with headache and sweats, followed by nausea and blowing off from both ends, if you get my drift.

I did not want anyone to know how sick I was. Thank God a couple of guys helped me and kept pumping water into me for three days. It all seems a foggy half memory now, but I know I was deathly sick and barely got all the paperwork completed before it was time for me to be transported to Saigon by helicopter.

I recall that I was shaky and weak but I wanted to get on an airplane and get out of Vietnam. The chopper ride seemed to last for an eternity. I don't recall looking out at the countryside, I just sat with my eyes closed, and concentrating on doing what I had to do to get through it all. I did my best to not let on how sick I was. I did not want to be put into a hospital only to end up a casualty of a rocket attack after surviving eight months of combat and almost four months on Nui Ba Den, not to mention getting overrun by Charlie. I needed to get home!

When I got to the point of checking out through Military Customs in Saigon they let me know that my paperwork was not in order and I ended up having to leave behind a lot of personal stuff collected while in Vietnam. At that point I was too weak to argue or try to give excuses. I said, "Just keep it and get me the hell out of here!"

That was that, the next day, DEROS day! I boarded a plane for home. The atmosphere on this flight was quite different from the somber flight that took me to Vietnam. There were lots of chatter and lots of stories being told on the flights home. Many friendships were made. I, however, was mostly quiet. I was starting to feel human again but I was still weak and worn out from the fever. I enjoyed the chatter and some stories and mostly the thought that in just a couple of days I would see my Gary Michael.... Thank you Lord for bringing me through it all!

Perhaps you are not done with me yet Lord. You have loads of work to do on me, I know I've been a challenge but I am yours.

Chapter 8
Victory Denied:

Vietnam 1959 – 1973

TRUE LIES — HIDDEN IN THE OPEN

The Vietnam War is declared officially ended but, when did the war actually begin? It is generally believed to have begun, when President John F. Kennedy authorized the U.S. military to send advisors to Vietnam in 1959. Actually direct U.S. involvement goes all the way back President Harry S. Truman's administration. June 30, 1950 President Truman sent 35 U.S. soldiers to Vietnam as "Military Advisors" for a war that was then known as the French Indochina War. July 26, 1950 Truman authorized 15 million dollars in military aid to the French. In September of 1950 Truman signed an approval for the Military Assistance Advisory Group (MAAG) to be deployed to Vietnam in order that MAAG would assist the French in the Indochina War. The President claimed they were not sent as combat troops, but to supervise the use of 10 million dollars worth of U.S. military equipment to support the French in their effort to fight the Viet Minh forces.

January 20, 1953 Dwight D. Eisenhower, former five-star Army general and Allied commander in Europe during World War II, is inaugurated as the 34th U.S. President. During his term, Eisenhower will greatly increase U.S. military aid and by 1954 the United States provided 80 percent of all war supplies used by the French. A cost, something to the tune of 3 billion dollars, was passed on to the American tax payers.

During the Eisenhower administration U.S. military advisors will continue to accompany American supplies sent to Vietnam. To justify America's financial commitment, President Eisenhower will cite a "Domino Theory" in which a Communist victory in Vietnam would result in surrounding countries falling one after another like a "falling row of dominoes." The Domino Theory will be used by a succession of Presidents and their advisors to justify ever-deepening U.S. involvement in Vietnam.

Early 1954 the commanding general of French forces in Indochina, General Henri Navarre, allowed the United States to send liaison officers to Vietnamese military forces. But it was too late, because of the siege and fall of Dien Bien Phu in the spring.

July 21, 1954 - The Geneva Accords divide Vietnam in half at the 17th parallel, with Ho Chi Minh's Communists ceded the North, while Bao Dai's regime is granted the South. The accords also provide for elections to be held in all of Vietnam within two years to reunify the country. The U.S. opposes the unifying elections, fearing a likely victory by Ho Chi Minh.

October 1954 - Following the French departure from Hanoi, Ho Chi Minh returns after spending eight years hiding in the jungle and formally takes control of North Vietnam.

In the South, Bao Dai has installed Ngo Dinh Diem as his prime minister. The U.S. now pins its hopes on anti-Communist Diem for a democratic South Vietnam. It is Diem, however, who predicts "another more deadly war" will erupt over the future of Vietnam.

Diem, a Roman Catholic in an overwhelmingly Buddhist country, encourages Vietnamese Catholics living in Communist

North Vietnam to flee south. Nearly one million leave. At the same time, some 90,000 Communists in the south go north, although nearly 10,000 Viet Minh fighters are instructed by Hanoi to quietly remain behind.

January 1955 - The first direct shipment of U.S. military aid to Saigon arrives. The U.S. also offers to train the fledgling South Vietnam Army.

As stated by the Geneva Accords, France was forced to surrender the northern half of Vietnam and to withdraw from South Vietnam by April 1956.

By the summer of 1957 U.S. Army Special Forces teams were sent to Nha Trang to set up a Vietnamese Special Forces training school.

In October of 1957 thirteen members of MAAG were wounded in a terrorist bombing in Saigon. More than likely the "terrorists" were actually Viet Cong.

FIRST AMERICAN CASUALTIES IN VIETNAM

On July 8, 1959 Major Dale Buis and Master Sergeant Ovnand became the first Americans to die in the Vietnam War during a Viet Cong attack on Bien Hoa, north of Saigon. Later that same year seven more Americans would die. The Viet Cong, otherwise known as the National Liberation Front, were formed in 1960. Kennedy became President in 1961.

By 1960 U.S. Special Forces had trained more than 50 units of Vietnamese Rangers. Although this aspect of the advisory experience began in the Eisenhower presidency, it was greatly expanded later under the keen interest and direction of President John F. Kennedy.

The Vietnam War officially ended on January 23, 1973, or so it had been declared by the government of the United States. It was much the talk of the media and in private circles. The general sentiment of the populace of the U.S. was a sigh of relief that it was finally over and no more young men would have to die. The draft had officially ended. The last combat troops had been pulled out of Vietnam. The sentiments of the general populace did not take into account the many lives that would be taken over the next many years.

By early 1974 North Vietnamese forces had increased greatly in numbers. President Nguyen Van Thieu announces a renewal of the war. Communists begin a major push to overthrow the South Vietnamese government; many key areas fall to the Communist troops.

January 8, 1975 - NVA general staff plan for the invasion of South Vietnam by 20 divisions is approved by North Vietnam's Politburo. By now, the Soviet-supplied North Vietnamese Army is the fifth largest in the world. It anticipates a two year struggle.

January 1975 President Gerald Ford states in a speech delivered in New Orleans that as far as the United States is concerned the war in Vietnam is "finished." Ford expresses the unwillingness of the U.S. to re-enter the war, reneging on the promise to help the South if the NVA violate the treaty.

March 13, 1975 - President Thieu decides to abandon the Highlands region and two Northern provinces to the NVA. This results in a mass exodus of civilians and soldiers, clogging roads and bringing general chaos. NVA then shell the disorganized retreat which becomes known as "the convoy of tears."

April 30, 1975 "the fall of Saigon"; the country came under Communist control, the reunification of the North and South of Vietnam begins to take place. As the National Assembly meets in July of 1976, the Socialist Republic of Vietnam names Pham Van Dong its prime minister. Van Dong and his fellow government leaders, all but one of whom are former North Vietnamese officials, take up residence in the nation's new capital—Hanoi. Saigon is renamed Ho Chi Minh City.

There was a literal blood bath that was about to occur throughout South Vietnam. That blood bath would be vengeance sought out against anyone and everyone, young and old, all who supported the government of the Democratic Republic of Vietnam. There were to be many more casualties of the war. They were the forgotten veterans of the war, both American and Vietnamese soldiers.

There had been a peace treaty signed, but in reality it was only pieces of paper that were of no value to the freedom fighters of South Vietnam and to the forgotten and broken soldiers who had fought and bled and died for a cause that had become a mockery played out by our liberal and biased media. The agreement didn't even warrant being called a "Treaty" it was deemed the Paris Peace Accords. To this day it evokes strong feelings in most Americans who are old enough to remember war and in those of us who experienced the horrors of combat in the war.

Up Close and Personal

They call it "The Golden Age of the 60s." Those years brought many new waves of technology, creativity, and innovation. The most memorable of the changes to me were the changes in our society, mainly one of rebellion. In my opinion our society has continued on a downward moral and ethical spiral ever since those "enlightening" times.

It also was the first time in history that the horrors of war were brought right into our living rooms. Night after night pictures and film footage were broad cast, bringing the Vietnam War and its carnage right up close and personal.

I would argue that many of us who lived through those years of the Vietnam War will never forget and are forever changed, regardless of what their opinion of the war was. The evening news did its level best to make us aware some of the horrible atrocities that occurred, things that should not have happened…. things that were against the rules of war. I'll never forget being told, "Don't make waves."

Today, on the subject of the wars in Afghanistan and Iraq, our liberal, left-wing news media has covered extensively the isolated cases of atrocity by U.S fighting forces, not much coverage is given to the torture or beheading of U.S soldiers, contractors, and reporters. Our media seems to be even more biased than they were during the Vietnam War. Perhaps it is because the media moguls of today were that college campus war protesters and draft dodgers of the Golden Age of the 60s.

Who can forget the My Lai massacre? As intended by the news media the My Lai incident is forever burned into the memories of all who read or watched the news of that time period. But what they didn't tell the American people was that such atrocities were commonplace in the North Vietnamese military. They would torture and kill anyone from the poorest village farmer to the local businessman who would not protect and support their cause. War is a vile and ugly thing, and horrible atrocities happen, they always have and always will. When young men, most fresh out of high school, see their buddies being killed all around them it's not hard to imagine that they could be overcome with hatred for the enemy, and how they would want to take revenge. Those young men faced death every day, never knowing when they themselves might be killed. War truly is Hell, a constant fight for survival, a matter of kill or be killed..... are you following me on this thought? I hope so for if you're not then you'd better check for a pulse or brain wave activity.

You may recall a famous black and white photograph that shows Nguyen Ngoc Loan, South Vietnam's national police chief executing a prisoner who was alleged to be a Viet Cong captain. His seemingly impromptu execution shocked millions around the world when the photograph was first published and it galvanized a growing antiwar sentiment in the United States, helping to hasten the change in the American public's view on the Vietnam War. Following the publication of that picture, Nguyen Ngoc Loan went on to become the symbol of war horror, branded by our liberal news media. The photographer, Eddie Adams won the 1969 Pulitzer Prize for Spot News Photography and a World Press Photo award for the photograph. I wonder if Eddie Adams ever photographed the bodies of Vietnamese civilians who had been tortured and murdered, their bodies on display at the entranceway to their Hamlet, hanged by the neck from poles or their lifeless bodies impaled on sharpened wooden stakes. They had been tortured and executed by Viet Cong militia then put on display as a warning to any and all villagers who resist their cause by supporting the freedom fighting ARVNs and U.S. Military.

How about another famous photo that served as a reminder of the horrors of the Vietnam War? The well-known photo has burned an indelible image into the minds of those who remember or experienced the Vietnam War. Photographer Nick Ut captured the photograph in 1972. The scene is that of children running down the middle of a highway, fleeing the village Trang Bang shortly after the South Vietnamese Air force had dropped Napalm bombs on their village destroying their homes. Trang Bang is located in Hau Nghia Province, South Vietnam. This horrifying image remembered is that of the naked young girl that appears in the center of the scene.

Kim Phuc, whose skin has been severely burned by the napalm, is fleeing her village along with the other children. What the accompanying news story failed to explain is that Viet Cong forces had retreated to the village, using the villagers as hostages, all the while still engaged in armed combat with ARVN forces. This was an all too familiar tactic of "Charlie." They would retreat to a defenseless village to use the villagers as "shields." If the villagers tried to escape the Viet Cong would shoot them in the back as they fled. It then comes down to a stand-off that can only be broken by an all-out attack. This photo illustrates the horrible aftermath of one such stand-off with the Viet Cong.

Kim Phuc is alive and well today, living in Canada with her husband and two children. In 1997, she passed the Canadian Citizenship Test with a perfect score, becoming a Canadian citizen. On June 30, 2008 National Public Radio broadcast her spoken essay, "The Long Road to Forgiveness", about her experience and life after that day.

This picture served fuel the already raging anti-war sentiments in the U.S. I suppose that Nick never had the opportunity to photograph a Hamlet that had been set ablaze by the NVA or the Viet Cong after they had slaughtered the villagers as well as all of the villagers' livestock. Or perhaps Nick never photographed the bodies of innocent children and women whose throats had been slit by Viet Cong because the villagers were not willing to risk hiding weapons caches for the VC and NVA. War is hell people!

Can "civilized" warfare exist? Has civilized warfare ever existed? I think not. The Vietnam War was lost because of politics and the "No Bomb" zones over North Vietnam. The war was lost because of public sentiment that was fueled by the lop-sided reporting of the war. People need to come to grips and accept the fact that WAR KILLS PEOPLE!! If you think that our adversaries will not kill innocent people because it goes against their ethics, you are living in the land of make believe and you need to resume taking your medication. There IS NO CIVILITY in warfare!!

Oh, and by the way, lest I forget to tell you a little tidbit of truth here. The picture of the children running from the village after the napalm bomb was dropped….. the newspapers forgot an important fact about the incident, the bomb was dropped by a Vietnam Air Force (VNAF) pilot flying a Sky-Raider A-1H. If the VC did not besiege Trang Bang, South Vietnam's Air force would not have bombed Trang Bang, and Kim Phuc would not have caught on fire. The one whom should be blamed on in this incident was the Vietnamese communists, NOT South Vietnam's Air Force or the Americans.

We, my friends, were denied a military victory in Vietnam as well as a hero's welcome home after the war, something that had never happened before in America. Young military men from all branches of the service were treated as if THEY were unpatriotic, as if THEY were wrong for serving their country when called. They saw draft dodgers and deserters, cowards and treasonists pardoned and given a free pass. They have even seen persons who blatantly committed acts of treason elected to our United States Senate.

If I hadn't experienced the venomous hatred as I traveled home after having just being discharged from active duty I would have had a difficult time believing that so many Americans could have been guilty of such an injustice. On my final trek home to Illinois, my flight took me from Los Angeles to Memphis Tennessee. While walking thru the airport to catch my connecting flight I experienced a surprising and unprovoked attack from a malicious, shrieking young woman who spat upon me while screaming at the top of her lungs, "Baby Killer, Baby Killer". The wrong that was done those to brave men is a wrong that can never be undone, however, there is hope.

HOPE AND FORGIVENESS

"To hope is to believe in humanity and in its future. Hope remains the heist reality, the age-old power; hope is at the root of all the great ideas and causes that have bettered the lot of humankind across the centuries.— Ronald Reagan –

But.... even greater than the hope expressed by one of my heroes, President Ronald Reagan, is the hope that lies in forgiveness! Stay with me on this one and I think I can make some sense of how this relates to those of us who served in Vietnam and how it relates to those who felt resentment for our government and the soldiers who fought a war that many thought was unjust.

I believe forgiveness is a choice we make as a result of our deeply committed faith, motivated by obedience to God and His command to forgive. Most of us never received a hero's welcome home. We returned to our families and our communities and there was little to no fanfare for us. Some of us even felt guilty that we had returned to the real world, leaving our friends and comrades behind in Vietnam. Many of us are still angry about the way we were treated by our government and our society. Anger and resentment is something that makes us smaller, but forgiveness is something that forces us to grow beyond where we have been. We need to choose to let go of the past. I recall a saying that has stuck in my mind, I wish I had been wise enough to be able to claim it for my own; "The stupid neither forgive nor forget; the naive forgive and forget; the wise forgive but do not forget."

Everyone says that forgiveness is a lovely idea until he has something to forgive. —C.S. Lewis—

Forgiveness is something God does for us, and we do for others as an act of grace. In the forgiving of others, we are also cancelling any indebtedness that we might believe others should feel toward us. We are canceling our obligation to carry the load of the hurt, anger, and isolation that we feel.

Corrie Ten Boom is a Christian woman who survived a Nazi concentration camp during the Holocaust, said, *"Forgiveness is to set a prisoner free, and to realize the prisoner was you."*

We will know the work of forgiveness is complete when we experience the freedom that comes as a result. We are the ones who suffer most when we choose not to forgive.

There is another important point I want to make in the forgiveness process. We, those who served in Vietnam, must forgive ourselves. We fought in a war that, to say the least, was unpopular with most Americans who were alive during the war. I believe ours was a just cause.

The Bible instructs us to forgive as the Lord forgave us:

Bear with each other and forgive whatever grievances you may have against one another. Forgive as the Lord forgave you. — Colossians 3:13

Is it okay to feel angry for an injustice that has been done to you? This question presents another reason to pray for the person or the system that we feel is indebted to us. We can pray for God to deal with the injustices, for God to judge them, and then we can leave that prayer at the altar. We no longer have to carry the anger and resentment. Although it is normal for us to feel anger toward sin and injustice, it is not our job to judge the other person in their sin.

Do not judge, and you will not be judged. Do not condemn, and you will not be condemned. Forgive, and you will be forgiven. — Luke 6:37

Why must we forgive? The best reason to forgive is because Jesus commanded us to forgive. We learn from Scripture, if we don't forgive, neither will we be forgiven:

For if you forgive men when they sin against you, your heavenly Father will also forgive you. But if you do not forgive men their sins, your Father will not forgive your sins. — Matthew 6:14-16

Chapter 9
Ours Was a Just Cause

I have to tell you… this chapter has been the most difficult of all for me to write. I actually began this chapter almost one year ago. I have suffered bouts writer's block at times during the writing of this book, but this chapter has challenged me to dig deep.

I have thought, searched, and researched in attempts to find any positive outcomes of this war. I have tried to put on paper, something that was affirmative for our country and our soldiers, those men and women who served bravely in Vietnam, I could not find anything that clearly stood out as a positive. I tried to find any positive influences on the Republic of South Vietnam and the brave ARVN soldiers, abandoned by our government, who fought valiantly to preserve their democratic republic. They were forsaken, left to be persecuted by the armies of communist North Vietnam. Many lost their lives as the NVA steamrolled through the south and ultimately crushed any resistance as they took control.

My inability to put a positive spin on the outcome of the war had been due to my misdirected focus on a socioeconomic outcome of the war. I was looking for visible positive influences on the people of South Vietnam that came as a result at our country's tragic experiment in setting up a democratic government for the people of South Vietnam, a people who I believe, we misunderstood. I believe many if not most of them just wanted to just be left alone; Left alone to recover from the decades of war that they suffered from during the French Indochina war.

Still I could find none, other than perhaps that the agony of the war had stopped once the south fell to the invaders from the north, their fellow countryman with an ideology that differed from the "powers that be" of the South Vietnamese government. Don't forget for one minute though, the war ended for the United States of America. Many of the activists opposed to the war, have calmed down and gone back to life as usual. Others who opposed the war have probably found another social injustice to march against. The people of Vietnam who backed the struggle for freedom in any way, they continue to this day to be persecuted by the Communist government of the unified Vietnam.

Few people who have grown up in these United States know the agonies of war in the way that the people of South Vietnam experienced it, up close and personal. The average peasant villager seemed to be ignored by both sides. Their hopes and dreams were ignored. Any lost of property or life in a rural village was nothing more than collateral damage. The villagers and farmers prayed for relief but their prayers went unanswered for years. All the while their prayers were probably to just be left alone, spared the consequences of the war that were thrust upon them.

HOPEFUL RESULTS

In an earlier chapter I mentioned that I was fortunate to have gotten to know the people of Vietnam in a way that most soldiers did not. The people of Vietnam were not just faces to me, these people had names, and they were real people that I served with, lived with, fought beside and on many occasions shared meals with in their villages and homes. They were genuine people with stories, with hopes and desires. They wanted a better life for themselves and for their children... just like us.

For them a possible positive result is that the war ended and they no longer have to live in fear of their village being overrun in the middle of the night. No longer to they have to anguish over the likelihood of having their wives and daughters raped, their sons being kidnapped and forced to serve an army that showed them no mercy, an army that had no regard for their life. The men of those villages no longer have to live in shame because they are powerless to protect their wives, daughters, and sons from an enemy who would slip into their villages under cover of night to slit the throats of those who resisted.

The Vietnamese were certainly victims of the war, but there were and are other victims of the hostilities of those days gone by. There are thousands of others who are victims, casualties of that war. From time to time our lives intersect with their lives. Sometimes we come uncomfortably close with those people. They seem to have no rudder in life, they're lost and broken. They could be conspicuously standing on a median near a traffic light. We try our best to ignore them, not making eye contact because that would make us feel even more uncomfortable than we already do because of their presence. Sometimes we don't give them a second thought, other times we might have an attack of conscience and hand them a buck or two. Whew, don't we feel better now as we drive away?

Who are the homeless veterans? The U.S. Department of Veterans Affairs (VA) says the nation's homeless veterans are mostly males (four percent are females). The vast majorities are single, most come from poor, disadvantaged communities, 45 percent suffer from mental illness, and half have substance abuse problems. America's homeless veterans have served in World War II, Korean War, Cold War, Vietnam War, Grenada, Panama, Lebanon, Operation Enduring Freedom (Afghanistan), Operation Iraqi Freedom, or the military's anti-drug cultivation efforts in South America. 47 percent of homeless veterans served during the Vietnam Era. More than 67 percent served our country for at least three years and 33 percent were stationed in a war zone.

How many homeless veterans are there? Although accurate numbers are impossible to come by — no one keeps national records on homeless veterans — the VA estimates that 131,000 veterans are homeless on any given night. Approximately twice that many experience homelessness over the course of a year. Conservatively, one out of every three homeless men who is sleeping in a doorway, alley or box in our cities and rural communities has put on a uniform and served this country. According to the National Survey of Homeless Assistance Providers and Clients (U.S. Interagency

Council on Homelessness and the Urban Institute, 1999), veterans account for 23 percent of all homeless people in America.

Wow! Those statistics are shocking and saddening. What can we do to help these "less fortunate souls" as we refer to them? We may volunteer at soup kitchens preparing or serving them meals. Did you know that many of the full-time volunteers at those soup kitchens and homeless shelters are veterans; former addicts and homeless people themselves? Many of them are "Saints" who realized that they need Jesus and that without His presence in their lives they would probably be dead, victims of an overdose or just plain over abuse of their bodies.

LOCKED AWAY

There are still other casualties, people we come in contact most every day. They are the less conspicuous veterans who have also been wounded by the war. They hide their wounds by locking away those memories of the horrors of combat. It is easier to bottle it up and just try to forget it. I am a living example of a person who did just that for years and years, until that day during my daughter's senior year in high school when I began putting pen to paper, recalling and recording some of the thoughts I had fought so long to erase from my memory. I was one of those who thought I was unaffected by Vietnam. I felt that those walking wounded who made themselves conspicuous by their inability to cope should "just get over it."

I felt that they needed to find something other than the war to blame their problems on. In my mind, chances were that they would have had problems in life anyhow and the Vietnam War was just another way of shirking their responsibilities. I was wrong to be so unfeeling.

My life has been transformed in a positive way by the combat experience. You might be asking yourself how that could be. I will explain and I hope you catch my meaning. I had learned as a child to bottle up my feelings, just lock them away and forget them and all would be well. I believe that attitude helped me to handle tragedy. It prepared me, so to speak, to cope with the horror and savagery of war. When I came home it was "end of story", on to another chapter in life. Another thing that attitude did for me was to harden my feelings. That made it easy for me to dismiss veterans who had been broken by the combat experience. In my mind, they just simply needed to cope and if they couldn't cope that was their problem. To me they were just winey "losers." I could dismiss them and ignore them with indifference. If by chance I came in close contact with them it was easy for me to ignore them and discount them as a human being of worth.

I will recall for you an incident I still regret to this day, the incident is mentioned in chapter 6. It was one of those times when the path of my life and the path of one of those unfortunate souls would cross. He was a Vietnam veteran standing near the Vietnam War Memorial, "The Wall." He held a piece of cardboard with words scribbled on it, it read *"Vietnam vet, homeless, please help."* I should have ignored him, which is normally what I would have done. I guess it was because of the moment; I had just looked up a name in the memorial directory, the name of a good and dear friend who I had served with. As I approached the wall I caught a glimpse of this guy with the sign. I turned toward him, hesitating for a brief moment, then I walked right up to him standing almost nose-to-nose with him and I said, "I'm a Vietnam vet too, why don't you just get over it." He stared at me in what appeared to be a mixture of shock and embarrassment. I turned and walked away feeling all smug and self-satisfied. I did not give that incident much thought after that day, until....

Believe it or not, that right there, at that point was the beginning of my transformation. However, I did not know at the time what had begun to take place. I had not asked for a transformation, but God had different plans for me and for my life. I would not realize for another 10 years, what had taken place. When I began the process of writing and remembering to prepare for a discussion/interaction about the Vietnam War with my daughter's senior high school history class, I recalled the incident at the Wall with the camouflage clad veteran who held the sign. I began to feel shame for my behavior, my inexcusable behavior. It was a new experience for me; I had never felt any compassion for the broken soldiers who had crossed my path.

I had been a hypocrite hiding inside of my privileged life. I attended church regularly and served on various committees over the years. I had performed as a heroic part-time/some-time volunteer reaching out to those who obviously needed

Jesus. All this time my heart and my emotions were trapped in that box with those terrible memories of the war. I closed off a part of who God had made me to be in the beginning. Suddenly and unexpectedly those feelings began to awaken. My "Grinch's Heart" two sizes too small, began to grow and compassion crept into my life... I wept.

I would not change back to the old me for the world. God commands us to, among other important things, love one another, to encourage one another, and to care for one another. I realized that I had been running from those feelings for as long as I can remember.

If there was hope for me.... there is hope for you. That hope lies in the hope that Jesus Christ promised us and by His blood we, you and me, are redeemed.

For in this hope we were saved. But hope that is seen is no hope at all. Who hopes for what he already has. – Romans 8:24—

Chapter 10
The Long Road Home

LOST AND FOUND

My sincerest hope is that this chapter will help to bring closure to those who have felt the pain of rejection, whether it be self-rejection or rejection by those close to us who have turned a virtual cold shoulder to our difficulties in life. Please don't think that these words I am speaking are words of cliché. I have felt some of the pain and rejection, perhaps in a smaller or greater way than you have. My hope is also that those who have or are actively turning the preverbal cold shoulder might read these words and find some degree of compassion for the one who struggles against the unseen demons that they cannot let go of. The operative word here is "cannot" versus "will not."

Those of us who are walking the long road home are suffering in a very real way. Our wounds are unseen to the eye but, and this is a very important "but"…. if you look at this person with an eye of compassion perhaps it will be revealed to you that the demons that relentlessly haunt their very lives ARE very real!

We cannot find that which was never lost.

RETURN

We cannot "*return*" if we have never "*turned.*" Now I can feel you asking yourself, "What is his point here?" My point is that when you have come to the end of yourself and you continue to struggle with the demons, you need something or someone else in your life. Whether you have walked away from a relationship with God or if you have never really had one, the point is that you need to turn your focus away from self and set your sites on God, for when we find ourselves at whit's end, out of resources, God will never fail us and He will set us free and heal our wounds.

If you have a Bible I suggest that you open it to the Old Testament, go the book of Hosea, it is toward the end of the Old Testament. Chapter 6, verse 1 says *"Come, let us return to the Lord, He has torn us to pieces" but he will heal us; he has injured us but he will bind our wounds.*

In other words the Lord will heal your wounds, but we must first "*turn/return*" to Him. So often in our lives when we have come to the end of ourselves we will pray to God to help us, deliver us from the giant we are facing or perhaps we will ask someone who we know prays to pray for us and our deliverance from our situation. Is it fair for me to point out that how can we expect God to help us if we only go to God in times of trouble, if we never take the small things in life to Him. How can we expect God to answer our prayers is we never give thanks for our blessings in life. The scripture in Hosea was written to point out the problem with a people who only call on God for deliverance, who only call on God to provide for them, a people who do not strive to live in a relationship with Him.

FINDING PURPOSE

Maybe you're one of those who feel broken. You've been treated poorly, you've been made to feel that you never measure up, that you're a loser, people have undervalued you, passed you by, and maybe you've ended up pretty hard and angry inside. But there is someone who has never thrown away a banged up or broken life, who sees beyond what's on the outside to the wounds on the inside and the potential He built into you when He made you. Jesus is your hope of a new beginning where the future doesn't have to be just an extension of a broken past.

Do you find that there is often a feeling of restlessness within you but you can't put your finger on a reason why you feel uneasy or on edge? Perhaps you are still looking for what your *purpose* is in this life. Consider this… God may be prompting your heart. Stay with me on this one and give it some thought. Have you prayerfully considered the fact that God is in pursuit of us? We often think that it is us that must seek Him out; we are the ones that must pursue God.

Are you familiar with Old Testament Bible stories? How did Abraham's relationship with God begin? Why did Moses go on a quest to lead the Israelites out of Egypt? How do all the stories in the Old and New Testaments begin? The common thread is that God always first made contact with them, God pursued them. What made the big difference is that when they had that feeling, whatever it was, they opened themselves up to it and God made contact with them.

Are you lost and looking for where you belong, perhaps Jesus is moving. Perhaps Jesus is pursuing you. Did you know that the name Jesus literally means, "Jehovah rescues." Jesus came to rescue us from the bondages of sin and to give us a Holy purpose in life. When we feel that life is hopeless, there is hope in Him. Remember that happiness is only for the moment but, the joy of the Holy Spirit is a feeling that comes to live within us when we surrender our lives to Jesus. Sin robs us of joy, and it condemns us to the death penalty of an awful eternity.

When we have those negative feelings of anger, depression, jealousy, and the list goes on. The best way to pull ourselves up and out of those feeling is to get our mind off of our self and to look outward toward others. There are many hurting people all around us and if we take steps to reach out and help others, suddenly our own negative feeling just seem to drift away.

Jesus risked His life to save us from a deadly situation from which we could never save ourselves. Maybe your heart has been restless to make a greater difference, and that is why. He is moving to rescue people you know from hopelessness. God is calling your name and saying, as He did to Moses, "So now, go, I am sending you." This is why He put you where you are - to rescue. Don't miss the destiny you were made for.

Don't be a superficial Christian, be sold- out for your faith in Christ. There are problems that you have come up against and you need to seek them out and defeat them, defeat the Vipers in your life.

It takes personal determination to defeat Satan. When you are headed in a direction that leads to positive change, personal trials will occur. Doing good doesn't always return reward. If when you reach out to help others you expect a thank you, you will often be disappointed. Don't lose heart; we are all on a pilgrimage. There challenges, find them, meet them, and defeat them. Shake off the enemy; the enemy is often inside of us. Personal blessings come for the common good.

Chapter 11
So What's the Take Away?

CONCLUSION

Much has happened in my life. When I look back I ask myself if there were things I would change. If I am absolutely honest with myself, the answer could only be yes. Through it all God has continued to enlighten the eyes of my heart to the truth of who He is and who He is in me;

(I pray also that the eyes of your heart may be enlightened in order that you may know the hope to which he has called you, the riches of his glorious inheritance in the saints,) — Ephesians 1:18

There have been times that I have strayed away from Him but He has faithfully led me back to the truth. Sometimes lessons have not been easy. I have not always been quick to recognize them as *Post Cards* from God. The longer we live our lives the less prone we are to adapt to change, but the more we mature in our relationship with God the more curious we should be to explore the infinite and the eternal mysteries of God. Even when I have recognized God's promptings I have not always been quick to respond. I will never forget what

God has taught me and because of that I will never be the same.

I want don't want to miss the opportunities God puts before me. I long to explore the things that I once had never even dreamed of, can you imagine what God, who has no boundaries, no limitations, could have in store for your future? We can experience them, the endless possibilities, only if we allow the God of the heavens to take hold of our dreams and turn them into reality.

Each of us has an idea of where we are in our spiritual lives and an indication of where we want to be, and more importantly, where God wants us to be. When we look at the gap between Him and us sometimes it is overwhelming. Of course we know that only Jesus can fill that gap. However, we have to ask ourselves the question, "Can we affect change in our character and thereby in our lives?" The resounding answer is NO! We can only affect change in our character if we surrender.... there's that word with the negative implication. The reason that surrender sounds so scary is, we give over control to someone other than ourselves and that idea is foreign to the human psyche.

You and I, each of us is a unique being. God has created us with a unique blend of gifts and talents. There is a special niche for you. Abide in Him, trust in Him and He will use you in ways you cannot imagine. The reality is that our lives, our human nature limits us to far more than we can ever imagine, but if we step out of our comfort zone and let God take control we can live out dreams that we may have never imagined. My favorite author, Erwin Raphael McManus wrote in his book "Wide Awake", "To imagine costs you nothing. Not to imagine could cost you everything." Go ahead, take the risk, you could live out the adventure of your life.

When we pray to God, asking His help or intervention or even take control, I believe there are at least 5 ways He will answer our prayer: YES, NO, WAIT, GROW, and NOT THAT WAY. God does answer prayer. All too often there are too many distractions in our lives and we do not recognize that He has answered us. But, God's solutions and answers don't always fit into our perspective. We limit Him in our minds, don't we? Would you want to serve a god whose intellect and imagination is equal to yours?

You and I are lousy at controlling our lives; we have proven it time and time again. Think about the last time you bungled a situation or made a wrong choice. Who was in control?

Trust in Him and He will produce fruit in your life that will absolutely amaze you. Through the virtues of self-control and faithfulness God will lead you and protect you.

God is asking you to make a commitment to walk with Him each and every day. He is not asking you to rededicate your life to Him. He is not asking you to make yet another resolution to change. He is asking you to surrender and trust in Him.

God wants only good for you. He will not slide into the driver's seat until you give Him permission. Revelation 3:20 Jesus says, "*Behold, I stand at the door and knock. If any man hears my voice and open the door, I will come in to him, and will sup with him, and he with me.*" These words are beautifully illustrated in artist, Holman Hunt's popular painting entitled "The Light of the World," it proclaims the heart of the Christian revelation. The artist's work pictures Jesus standing at the door of the human heart. In His hand is a lantern which represents the light of our conscience. The light reveals sin as it shines upon the door with rusty hinges and barred with nails. The door is also entwined with brambles, vines, and grass, symbolizing man's earth-bound nature. Profoundly important is the fact that no outside latch or knob is visible, revealing that the door can only be opened from the inside. Jesus knocks; He cannot come in until the door is opened with an invitation to come in.

Once you surrender control to God you will begin to see a transformation in attitude. You will begin to experience the true joy of the Holy Spirit. You will actually begin to see the gap closing between where He wants you to be and where you know you are. Your dreams of living a life in Him and for Him begin to develop into a reality you had never imagined. You are no longer held captive by the things of the world that once glittered and excited you.

Remember how it is that God made you. Your deeper instinct is to be alive, not just live! My friends, you will begin to live free. Free to be what God created you to be. Free to explore and experience a life that you had only dreamed of. Free to serve, free to experience the wholeness and richness of the Spirit filled life.... free to "Live out Loud!"

Jim - 詹
姆
斯

Would you like to see your manuscript become a book?

If you are interested in becoming a PublishAmerica author, please submit your manuscript for possible publication to us at:

acquisitions@publishamerica.com

You may also mail in your manuscript to:

**PublishAmerica
PO Box 151
Frederick, MD 21705**

www.publishamerica.com

CPSIA information can be obtained at www.ICGtesting.com
Printed in the USA
BVOW021301171011

273841BV00001B/5/P

9 781462 641239